MARRIAGE
FITNESS

Praise for MARRIAGE FITNESS

"Once in awhile, I come across a book that can really make a difference... This is one of those times. MARRIAGE FITNESS will not only improve your marriage significantly, but I believe you will become a better individual by following its guidelines. With marriages falling apart all around us, this timely book can and will _work_!"

–Dr. Stephen R. Covey, author
The 7 Habits of Highly Effective People

"A breakthrough for the institution of marriage. This should be required reading for every spouse in America."

–David J. Lieberman, Ph.D.
New York Times Bestselling Author, *Make Peace with Anyone*

"Deeply rooted in psychology, theology, and the pragmatic realities of day-to-day living, MARRIAGE FITNESS—like the best exercise regimen—increases stamina, flexibility, and overall well-being. MARRIAGE FITNESS offers a step-by-step, wonderfully practical way to strengthen, revive, or rejuvenate any marriage."

–Dr. Richard J. Levin
Author of *Shared Purpose*

"Mort Fertel does a wonderful job explaining the root of marriage success, organizing a clear plan to achieve it, and interweaving fascinating stories as well as his own personal journey to make MARRIAGE FITNESS a pleasure and a power."

–M. Gary Neuman, M.S., LMHS
Author of *Emotional Infidelity*

"Excellent! Great 'marriage' of theory and practice...Mort Fertel's comprehensive book is a practical, hands-on approach to gaining and maintaining the love we all want . . ."

–Michael Adamse, Ph.D.
Author of *Anniversary: A Love Story* and *Affairs of the Net*

"MARRIAGE FITNESS is a valuable and sophisticated psychological tool for empowering and enhancing marriage. Mort Fertel sheds light on 'Love'; a concept too often misrepresented by mainstream psychology as esoteric or vague. He then elevates the paramount driving force of 'Love' in an exceedingly spirited and practical way, giving the reader new hope, new direction, and a new set of techniques to overcome the challenges of marriage. This book will take your marriage to new heights of clarity, intimacy and connectedness beyond your wildest dreams!"

–Dr. Brian Greer
The Center for Family Development
Diplomate American Boards of Child &
Adult Psychiatry and Neurology

"MARRIAGE FITNESS is a splendid, must-read text providing those in significant yet challenged relationships a true opportunity to relocate and protect the charm and spirit in their lives. MARRIAGE FITNESS is among the most enjoyable and pragmatic 'relationship-saving workouts' that I have had the pleasure to review. Taken seriously with meticulous attention paid to the detail of its broad genre of relevant exercises, there exists little doubt that many couples will find excitement and exhilaration re-establishing and supporting the love in their lives."

–Robert L. Hersh, Psy.D.

"MARRIAGE FITNESS is practical and enjoyable. It offers a step-by-step plan for a strong and healthy marriage and the stories make it a joy to read. Mort Fertel is highly motivating—he'll inspire you get your marriage in top shape!"

–Ashira Bunder Drury, M.S. Ed.

"The premise of MARRIAGE FITNESS gives an entirely new meaning to 'self help'!"

–Jill Oppenheimer Kaplan, Ph. D.

"Mort Fertel has formulated the best plan for marriage I have ever seen. His research is extensive, his approach practical, and I guarantee he'll inspire you to action."

–Elyse Hurtado, Ph.D.

"MARRIAGE FITNESS sets the standard upon which all future relationship success strategies will be measured. Bravo!"

–Rebecca Carner, Ed.D.
Diplomate Neuropsychology

"Mort Fertel draws masterfully from diverse wisdoms and synthesizes the best ideas on relationship success into a clear and compelling message. MARRIAGE FITNESS incorporates the wisdom of psychology and theology, and utilizes some of history's greatest thinkers including Einstein, Plato, Sophocles, Emerson, and Oliver Wendell Holmes. Mort Fertel blends all that with fascinating stories, a children's tale, and his own personal journey. This is a book that *everyone* can relate to."

–Allen Segal, Ph.D.

"This is the only book of its kind. A standing ovation for Mort Fertel."

–Melissa Rosenberg, MSS, NHA

"MARRIAGE FITNESS provides a well conceived plan based on love and alliance that gives life to the institute of marriage threatened by today's culture."

–Ambassador David M. Walters

MARRIAGE FITNESS

4 Steps to Building & Maintaining Phenomenal Love

By Mort Fertel

MarriageMax, Inc.
Baltimore, MD
www.MarriageMax.com

Marriage Fitness
4 Steps to Building & Maintaining Phenomenal Love

DISCOUNT BULK PURCHASES
This book is available at special discounted prices for all bulk purchases including sales promotions, education, premiums, fundraisers, and gifts. Special editions, including personalized covers or imprints, can be printed for quantities of 500 and more. For more information, please visit www.MarriageMax.com.

First printing 2004.

Permission granted by Southern Days Music to use "looking for love in all the wrong places."

He Touched Me
Lyric by Ira Levin
Music by Milton Schafer
(c) 1965, 1966 (Renewed) IRA LEVIN and MILTON SCHAFER
All Rights Controlled by EDWIN H. MORRIS & COMPANY, A Division of MPS Communications, Inc.
All Rights Reserved

Although the author and publisher have made every effort to ensure the accuracy and completeness of the information contained in this book, we assume no responsibility for errors, inaccuracies, omissions, or any inconsistency herein.

Book design by Fine Line Design
Cover design by George Foster
Author photograph by Paul Kline
Edited by Shannon M. Dougherty

Fertel, Mort.
    Marriage fitness : a revolutionary system for
building phenomenal love, including the MarriageMax
4-step plan / by Mort Fertel.
    p. cm.
    LCCN 2003116636
    ISBN 0-9744480-0-1

    1. Marriage. 2. Man-woman relationships. 3. Love.
I. Title.

HQ734F47 2004   646.7′8
                     QBI33-1758

MarriageMax, Inc.
Baltimore, MD
www.MarriageMax.com

For my wife, Ari.
You complete me.

ACKNOWLEDGEMENTS

The greatest thing we can do for our children is to improve ourselves. I want to thank my four beautiful children for inspiring me to learn how to succeed in love and marriage. I love you so much.

Thank you, Mom. I feel a deep sense of purpose in life and the confidence to pursue it. Both are a gift from you. Thank you for your continual support, encouragement, and love.

Dad, thank you for everything you have done for me and taught me.

Sonny, you make loving look so easy. You embody traits I struggled a lifetime to acquire. The older I get, the more I appreciate who you are and what you have done for me. Thank you.

Thanks, Melissa, for taking time out of your busy life to review the manuscript and offer your insights. I appreciate your involvement and all the ways you found to help.

Arthur and Julie, thank you for your deep concern, passionate efforts, and careful reading of every version of the manuscript. From the first draft to the final proofing, you were there for me. I appreciate all your help. Most of all, thank you for Ari.

Noah, thank you for your help. You always find a way to make a difference. Do you realize that the seeds for this book were planted when we met more than twenty years ago?

To my amazing and dear friends: Steve Hartman, Sue Kaskel, Betty and Ephraim Goldberg, Dov Linzer, Hadassah

Field, and Jody Bennett—thank you so much for your unselfish help and loyal friendship. Your feedback was instrumental in refining and shaping the manuscript.

Elyse, thank you for all the ways you found to make a difference. No matter where I was with the project—no matter what I needed—you were there to help. Through your efforts, and by involving others, you made a huge contribution. I am deeply grateful.

Thank you, David Aaron. Your insights are an inspiration and your wisdom is profound. May you continue to bring light to the world. I will always be thankful for the impact you had on my life.

Thank you, Randee Dutton. I was overwhelmed by how much time and effort you put into improving the manuscript. I hope you know how much I valued your perspective.

Thank you, Jill Kaplan and Kathy Williams, for investing so much time and energy into offering your input.

Many thanks to my editor, Shannon M. Dougherty. You are a consummate professional and a pleasure to work with. You identified some key issues and pushed me to make the book better. Thanks for a job well done.

Mordechai Neuman, I owe you a lifetime of thanks. So much in my life, including this book, would never have happened without your help and wisdom.

And most of all—to the love of my life, Ari. We became this book. I am so blessed to have you as my wife. I love you more than words can say.

Finally, all my gratitude to The Author—it is my honor and privilege to serve as Your pen.

TABLE OF CONTENTS

Part II: The MarriageMax™ 4-Step Plan

Introduction

We all have a story about how we fell in love. Do you remember your story?

Unfortunately, most of us have a story about how we fell *out* of love too. For some couples the impetus was financial stress, a challenging child, the loss of a loved one, an affair, an addiction, an accident, an illness, an obsession, or unresolved issues from the past.

Maybe you can't identify a specific cause but instead are victim to time and life which ate away at the special spark you and your spouse once had.

Whatever your situation, it's likely that your relationship is not what it used to be.

What are you going to do?

Half of married couples call it quits. The other half settle for being roommates. Only a small percentage of couples are in love after a few years of marriage. It's no wonder everyone says "love is a mystery."

Love is NOT a mystery!

There are specific things you can do with your spouse to create love in your marriage and to maintain your love for a lifetime.

Just as there are physical laws of the universe (such as gravity), there are also laws for love. Just as the right diet and exercise program makes you physically healthy, a certain way of life with your spouse will make your marriage strong. It's a direct cause and effect. If you know and apply the laws, the results are predictable—you can "make" love.

MARRIAGE FITNESS offers you a step-by-step system to make and maintain love in your marriage. The program can work for any couple. And the best news is that you don't have to dig into your past, dredge up your problems, or practice communication techniques. This is not marriage therapy; it's *Marriage Fitness*.

A Surprising Solution

The wisdom in MARRIAGE FITNESS is a result of years of study and research, coaching couples, and conducting marriage seminars. But unlike other relationship experts who approach marriage from a clinical perspective, for me the topic of relationship success is also very personal.

Do you remember I said that every couple has a story about how they fell *out* of love? I'd like to share with you the story of my marriage.

My wife and I started out deeply in love—like most couples. We stayed up all night talking, surprised each other with thoughtful gifts, and spoke to each other in code words. You know the feeling of really being connected? That was us.

But then something happened that destroys most marriages. We had a son who died when he was just one week old. And then we had twin daughters, who also died as newborns. In less than two years, we lost three children.

Understandably, my wife became depressed. I tried to cope by immersing myself in work. We ran from each other emotionally, quickly becoming roommates instead of soul mates.

Everything felt different. Instead of talking to each other all night, it became a chore to talk for a few minutes. Instead of using our code words, sometimes we resorted to using curse words.

It wasn't long before we began to think: Is this what it's going to be like for the next fifty years? Is this what we had in mind when we married? Will we ever again anticipate a phone call from the other or fantasize in the middle of the day? Will we ever resolve the problems we constantly fight about? What about true love?

We didn't want to lose each other so we made a commitment to work on our marriage. We tried the obligatory, "Honey, let me repeat what you said to make sure I understood you correctly." We also learned about gender differences and applied conflict-resolution strategies. We even went to therapy to wrestle with our problems. But guess what? To our deep disappointment, nothing *really* changed.

You might say our marriage improved. We understood each other better, communicated more effectively, and solved a few problems. We became better roommates, but we did not become soul mates again. And our core problems remained unchanged.

Then we had a breakthrough. We decided to *set aside all our problems* and focus on *connecting* with each other. We used a series of "exercises" that created a union—an emotional togetherness—which transformed our marriage. Not only did we resolve our differences, we fell in love again! And we did it—not by dealing with our problems (as serious as they were)—but by establishing healthy habits in our marriage.

This is the solution to most marital situations—to step away from your problems and spend your time and energy building your relationship through positive actions.

It's counter-intuitive, but if you strengthen your relationship, most of your problems will dissipate and what remains of them can be more easily addressed in a safer, softer, and more forgiving marital environment.

Many couples complain that the worst day of their week is the day they go to therapy together. They're not getting along and the one night a week they spend together is spent with their arms folded and their legs crossed in opposite directions immersed in the negativity of their marriage. I remember leaving our sessions feeling hopeless and frustrated.

If your marriage is stressed, it's NOT the time to tackle difficult issues. In fact, if the timing is not right, trying to solve problems with your spouse can damage your marriage and make it *less likely* that you'll ever find resolution.

If you have back problems, sometimes the solution is to do sit-ups. Strengthening one part of your body can heal another. Your marriage works in a similar way.

How to Simplify Your Situation

The transformation of my marriage and my disappointment with traditional counseling inspired my exploration into the topic of marriage success.

I read virtually every relationship book on the market. I discovered that relationship success literature focuses primarily on conflict-resolution and communication skills. It's surprising how much is written about solving problems and communicating more effectively, and how little is written about how to create love.

MARRIAGE FITNESS is fundamentally different from any other book about relationship success. MARRIAGE FITNESS is not about conflict-resolution or communication skills because these are NOT the keys to a successful marriage.

If a doctor cures your illness, does that mean you're healthy? No! It just means you're not sick. Similarly, solving your marital problems will NOT create love in your relationship. You might get along better and fight less, but you won't necessarily have a healthy marriage. And your problems will probably reappear or new ones will surface.

The irony of the conflict-resolution and communication approaches to love is that the correlation is backwards. Solving problems does not create love. It's love that solves problems. Effective communication does not create love. It's love that creates effective communication. The question to ask is *not* how to solve your problems or communicate effectively. The question is—how do you fall in love again? How do you make that magical connection and how do you make it last? That's the key to a successful marriage and that is what this book is about.

In his essay "The Hedgehog and the Fox," based on an ancient Greek parable, Isaiah Berlin describes how different people approach problems. Some people are like foxes; they know many things. Other people are like hedgehogs; they know one big thing.

A fox is a clever animal who devises many tactics for attacking the hedgehog. Everyday the fox has another brilliant strategy to win his prey.

The hedgehog, on the other hand, is a slow boring creature whose defense is the same no matter how the fox attacks.

Everyday the fox thinks, "Aha, now I've got you." But everyday, no matter how the fox approaches, no matter where he strikes, no matter what time of day he attacks, as soon as the hedgehog senses danger he thinks, "Here we go again," and he rolls up into a little ball, extends his sharp spikes, and spoils the fox's best laid plans.

Berlin explained that some people (foxes) make everything complicated. Their approach changes depending on the circumstances.

Other people (hedgehogs) simplify the complexity of the world into one principle—one basic idea that determines their every move.

Now don't misunderstand. Hedgehogs are not simpleminded. On the contrary, their understanding of the world is so profound that they're able to identify the most fundamental elements. Albert Einstein, Carl Marx, Sigmund Freud, Charles Darwin, and Adam Smith—they were "hedgehogs."

To succeed in your marriage, you must be a hedgehog too!

Every marriage has problems, issues, and challenges. But in every instance the solution is the same. The solution is love!

I know it sounds hokey, but think about when you fell in love? What problems did you have then? Hardly any, right?

Was it difficult to communicate when you fell in love? Of course not. And you didn't need communication techniques either. You barely needed words. You communicated with the wink of an eye and finished each other's sentences.

Love magically transforms everything.

You know the twitch in the corner of your spouse's mouth? Remember when you thought it was cute? Then one day it became annoying, right? Why?

Your spouse used to be thrifty and now your spouse is cheap. What changed?

The love in your marriage changed and that changed everything. And when you rebuild your love, everything will change again.

Don't get bogged down in the negativity of trying to solve your problems. It's not fun and it's not productive. Be a hedgehog. Use this Marriage Fitness program to build positive energy in your relationship. You will transform your marriage and solve your problems.

Two-in-One

MARRIAGE FITNESS offers insights into the inner-workings of love *and* a corresponding four-step action plan.

After you read Chapters 1 through 3, you'll experience a paradigm shift and understand the dynamics of your marriage better than ever before. You'll have a new frame of reference enabling you to pinpoint that magical connection known as love. Chapters 1 through 3 also explain the philosophy underlying Marriage Fitness and answer some crucial questions. What *really* is love? What's the solution to most marital problems? What does it mean to be soul mates?

After you read Chapters 4 through 7, you'll be empowered with a Marriage Fitness program called the MarriageMax™ 4-Step Plan.

The MarriageMax™ 4–Step Plan
1. Put Love First
2. Give Presence
3. Move from Me to We
4. Save Yourself

Chapters 4 through 7 are each devoted to one step of the MarriageMax™ 4-Step Plan. Each chapter explains how and why each step manifests love in your marriage. Most importantly, each chapter offers you exercises to strengthen your marriage and explains exactly how to apply each step.

By the time you turn the last page of MARRIAGE FITNESS, you'll understand the dynamics of your relationship and you'll know exactly how to apply your knowledge to create lasting love in your marriage.

Getting Your Marriage in Shape

Your marriage is the lead domino in your life. Whichever way it falls is the way everything else in your life goes too. That's one reason why it's so important to focus on your marriage. Not only because it's an awesome experience to be in love, but because being in love—having a healthy marriage—makes you a better parent, a more productive professional, and a healthier person spiritually, emotionally, and physically. *Your marriage affects your entire life.*

When you're in love, everything is wonderful. But when you're not, nothing is ever enough. You could dress in the latest fashions, go on every diet, make all the money in the world, and be a leader in your community, but if you're not connected with your spouse—if you're not at peace in your home—nothing will be right.

You may not realize the extent to which your fulfillment in life depends on your marriage. You may think your marriage is one aspect of your life that contributes to your overall happiness. It's not true. Your marriage is the framework—the very bedrock—upon which every aspect of your life is built. It's the pool in which everything swims. If it's healthy, everything thrives. If it's polluted, everything suffers.

Most people don't focus on their marriage until they have problems. But that's like ignoring your body until you're sick. Everyone knows that the key to good health is diet and exercise—a healthy lifestyle. It's the same with your marriage. Just as you need a healthy diet and exercise for your body, you need Marriage Fitness for your relationship.

This book offers you a straightforward do-it-yourself Marriage Fitness plan complete with everything you need to succeed.

Ideally, you *and* your spouse should read MARRIAGE FITNESS and work on the MarriageMax™ 4-Step Plan together. If your spouse is not interested in reading the book, ask your spouse to participate in the MarriageMax™ 4-Step Plan with your guidance. Even if your spouse does not participate, *you* can still strengthen your marriage using Marriage Fitness.

Consider the profound love you feel for your child. Is it because of everything they do for you? No. *You* created that love. It's a result of everything *you* do. In the same way, *you* control the love you experience in your marriage. Love is a verb. It's something *you* do.

A Tribute to Your Marriage

There's a story about a man; we'll call him Mr. Jones. He was at a dinner party with his wife when he was asked, "If you died, but could come back as anyone, who would it be?" Without hesitation Mr. Jones said, "I'd want to come back as Mrs. Jones' second husband."

What a compliment to his wife! What a tribute to their marriage!

So, how would you answer that question? And what would your spouse say?

Can you imagine you and your spouse answering that question just like Mr. Jones? It can happen. I'm not just offering you an okay marriage; I'm saying that just two short months from now, if you or your spouse had only one wish in another life, you would wish to be with each other.

What I'm offering you . . . is a *phenomenal* marriage— a truly healthy relationship!

No matter what state your marriage is in today, I believe you're 100% entitled to a strong marriage filled with passion, intimacy, and shared purpose.

You *can* keep up with the Jones'. MARRIAGE FITNESS will show you how.

Feel free to email me your comments and questions about MARRIAGE FITNESS, your experience with the MarriageMax™ 4-Step Plan, and any stories or insights you feel inspired to share. It would be an honor to hear from you.

Mort Fertel
MortFertel@MarriageMax.com
www.MarriageMax.com

Get FREE Marriage e-Help

Special Online Supplement
"How to Get Your Spouse to Change"
Available FREE at www.Marriagemax.com/Change.asp

PART I:
HOW LOVE WORKS

Chapter 1

THE POWER OF LOVE

O nce upon a time, a happy princess put on her bonnet and took a walk in the woods with her favorite ball. She stopped and sat on a rock next to a cool spring with a rose in the middle of it. One time she threw her ball in the air so high that it dropped and rolled into the water. The princess was very sad. She wept.

A frog poked his head out of the water and asked the princess, "Why are you crying?"

The princess whined, "My favorite ball fell into the water. I would give all my fine clothes, pearls, jewels, and everything I have in the world to get it back."

The frog said, "I don't want your fine clothes, pearls, jewels, or anything you have in the world. But if you invite me to your palace, let me eat at your table and sleep in your bed, and if you love me, I will bring you your ball."

"This is nonsense," thought the princess. "This silly frog can't leave the water. I'll agree to his wishes just to get my ball back." And so she did.

But as soon as the frog gave the princess her ball, she ran away as fast as she could. The princess didn't keep her word.

The next day, when the princess sat down for dinner, she heard a strange noise—tap, tap—plash, plash—as if something was coming up the marble staircase. Soon afterwards there was a gentle knock at the door, and a little voice cried out, "Open the door, my princess dear."

The princess ran to the door. When she opened it, she saw the frog that she had forgotten about. She screamed, "Go away," and slammed the door and ran back to the dinner table.

The king, her father, saw that she was upset and asked her what happened.

"There is an ugly frog at the door," she said. "Yesterday he got my ball from the spring. I promised him he could come to the palace, eat at the table, sleep in my bed, and I told him I would love him. I didn't mean it, but now he wants to come in."

The king said to the princess, "You must keep your word. Let him in and do as you promised."

So the princess let the frog into the palace and brought him to the dining room.

"Lift me upon the chair next to yours," said the frog to the princess, "and let me eat next to you."

The princess glanced toward the king, who gave her an insistent nod, and she lifted the frog and they ate together.

After his meal the frog said, "I'm tired. Carry me upstairs and put me in your bed."

The princess reluctantly took the frog upstairs and put him in her bed.

The princess was tired too, but she couldn't sleep. She knew she still had not fulfilled her promise. She had not loved the frog.

So the princess took a deep breath, closed her eyes, and kissed the ugly frog. When she opened her eyes, the princess was astonished to see a handsome prince instead of the ugly frog. The next day they married and lived happily ever after.

There is nothing in life that we pursue more passionately than love. We have many wants and needs, but nothing preoccupies our mind and dictates our actions like love. Our desire for love is at the bedrock of our existence. And believe it or not, *The Frog Prince* teaches us why.

In the beginning of *The Frog Prince,* the princess had

her ball and happiness. But she had not yet met a handsome prince. When she lost her ball and became sad, the frog, who knew he could become a handsome prince, offered her everything she wanted in life. All she had to do was love him and she would have her ball, happiness, and a handsome prince. But the princess wasn't willing to love the frog. So she got her ball, but became tangled in a frustrating relationship with the frog.

The princess tried to improve her situation by getting rid of the frog. She lied to him, ran from him, forgot about him, screamed at him, slammed the door in his face, and cringed at the thought of kissing him. None of that changed anything. But when she kissed him—when she loved him—that changed everything. The frog *became* the handsome prince and in the blink of an eye (literally) she had everything she wanted in life—her ball, happiness, and a handsome prince.

And so it is with love. It has a miraculous transformative power. When we're in love, everything changes "from frog to prince." *Love is like a golden lens through which we experience all of life.*

Marriage Fitness and the MarriageMax™ 4-Step Plan is based on the premise that there is nothing more important in your marriage or in your life than building phenomenal love between you and your spouse. Fixing problems, improving communication, understanding each other better—it all pales in comparison to the transformative effect of creating love. This chapter explains the transformative power of love. It explains how and why love is the solution to your relationship problems, the secret to effective communication with your spouse, and the path to ultimate fulfillment in your marriage and in your life.

Clarifying Your Needs

To get what you want, you have to know what you need. You experience longing and desire in life, but for what? You want—but *what* do you really want?

Did you ever get a food craving you couldn't satisfy? You go to the kitchen, scan the shelves of the refrigerator, and return to the couch empty-handed. A minute later you're back in the kitchen for a second look. Nothing changed, of course, but this time you pick something, even though it doesn't appeal to you. You eat it, but as expected, it wasn't what you wanted. So you return to the kitchen for a third time.

We've all had the experience of wanting something, but not knowing what we need to satisfy our desire.

At the root of our existence, what do we need? We want our needs met, but what is it that, once attained, would satisfy us? Where can we find ultimate fulfillment? What is our most primal desire, and what does it have to do with Marriage Fitness and creating phenomenal love in your life?

The Greek philosopher Plato described the existential root of human beings using a myth which portrays two people joined back-to-back—male and female—as one androgynous creature. Since man and woman could not face each other, Zeus sent a thunderbolt that split them into two. According to Plato, since man and woman were originally connected, we are instinctively motivated to return to that original state of connection.

The Bible describes human origin similarly. It says, "God created *him;* male and female He created *them.*" Why does the Bible first refer to man in the singular ("him") and then in the plural ("them")? Which is it? Did God create one person or two? The answer is "yes." Ancient tradition explains that God created man and woman back-to-back, as one androgynous person. Later God separated man and woman, but that original connection lies at the root of our existence and forms an indelible yearning for us to be connected again.

Not only do we inherit from the original human being a desire to connect (according to many traditions), but we crave it as a result of our own beginning too. From conception through birth, we're connected to our mother. Even after birth, research shows that we don't feel distinct from our mother even though our connection is no longer physical. The original connection with our mother contributes to form our consciousness which longs for connection.

Although we have a primal need to connect to someone else, nature doesn't allow us to be satisfied with our connection to our mother. In fact, nature seems to discourage it. As children, we gradually separate from our mother physically and emotionally.

I remember my son's first day at school. My wife and I were concerned that he wouldn't be able to separate from my wife who had been home with him for over three years. We drove him to school, walked him to his classroom, opened the door, and he ran to the center of the classroom where all the kids were playing. He didn't even say goodbye. We peered through the window of the door for a few minutes and watched him play. We cried. He did not.

Our first day of school is just one step in a long process of separation that leads to independence and autonomy. But the more independent we become, the more we realize how dependent we really are. In other words, the more we wean from the connection to our mother, the more we need to connect with someone else. Beginning with your teenage years, making that new connection probably became your most passionate concern.

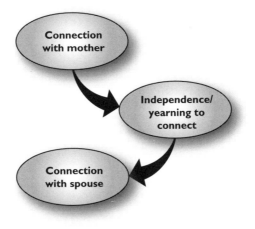

Your need to connect is primal. Ultimately, true love—a deep profound connection with another person—is the only solution to your most primal yearning.

The Greek playwright Sophocles said, "One word frees us of all the weight and pain of life. That one word is love." When it comes to love, it's all on the line. How else can we explain the things people do for love—things that sometimes make no sense.

The fact that you married at all in spite of the statistical probability of failure is illogical. That's because love is not logical; it's ontological. It's your most basic need. It's what you *really* want.

Falling in Love

Falling in love is the most euphoric experience in life. And now you know why. Love is a bond that quenches your primal need for connection. Falling in love is like finding the missing part you've been looking for your entire life. It completes you.

When my wife and I reconnected, everything broken became whole again. We experienced a quantum change in our marriage and in our lives. Something just clicked. Everything changed "from frog to prince."

Love transforms you. It puts a glow on your face and a hop in your step. If you're a workaholic, you'll take every vacation day you're owed. If you're shy, you'll come out of your shell. If you usually go to sleep early, you'll stay up all night talking. Love is a stimulant—look how it inspired poets, artists, storytellers, and philosophers for thousands of years.

Do you remember when you fell in love and your spouse was perfect? And you were perfect for each other, right? You may have even said things like, "I wouldn't want to change a thing."

If we asked most brides and grooms for a list of each other's flaws, I suspect the list would be short. Love is a golden lens through which your lover is flawless. Love makes everything right—and everything different. Do you know the feeling? I bet you do. But do you still *have* the feeling? You probably don't.

What happened? The person you would have died for is now the person you want to kill. Your spouse was the answer to everything and now he's your biggest problem. She made you happier than you'd ever been and now she is the source of all your misery.

Am I exaggerating your situation? Maybe you don't have major problems, but maybe you don't have much excitement either.

Regardless of your situation, two questions remain. What happened to that exhilarating experience? And how can you regain it?

At the risk of sounding clinical, research has shown that falling in love is a biochemical experience, which inevitably wears off like the fizz in a glass of soda. The initial connection you felt toward your spouse was real, but it was a natural phenomenon. You might not want to hear this, but what you thought was your romantic destiny was just nature taking its course.

When it comes to love, nature's course lasts about two years. After that, the connection fades. It could be that neither of you "did" anything, but everything will feel different. You may notice flaws in your spouse you never saw before. You've known each other for years, but you can't believe you didn't realize your spouse was _____. You wonder how you missed such blatant flaws—especially now that you know that everyone else saw them from the beginning. Why did it take you years to realize what everyone else knew all along?

After about two years together, you may experience new incompatibilities too. Things may not go as smoothly as they once did. It may be more difficult to get along. You may find it hard to believe that you were not aware of these incompatibilities earlier. How did you miss them?

As the natural connection fades from your marriage, so will that euphoric experience. This doesn't mean your marriage will crash. You may not even have major problems. But you won't have the profound love that you once did. What will you do then?

Choosing Love

When the original connection with your spouse fades, you have several options.

One option is to accept the situation, scale down your expectations, and try to navigate an arrangement that "works." Other than divorce, most couples choose this option.

How many couples do you know who are deeply connected and have a phenomenal marriage? Most couples are like partners dividing responsibility to satisfy each other's needs. A husband who is the financial engine and a wife who cares for the home and children is one of many possible scenarios. And although couples like this have bitter fights, harsh words, problems, frustrations, irreconcilable differences, and aggravation, they also enjoy sex, money, vacations, friends, children, companionship, and family celebrations.

This is a typical marriage—it includes the good and the bad. Some people in marriages like this are "happy." Others are not. Most fall somewhere in the middle. But none are experiencing the profundity of true love and the ultimate fulfillment of a phenomenal marriage.

A second option is to address the problems in your marriage by improving your understanding of yourself and your spouse, examining how you interact, and developing more effective communication and negotiating skills. This may solve some of your problems. You might communicate more effectively. You may not fight as often, and when you do, it may be more controlled and constructive. You may negotiate a more compatible, bearable, even pleasant existence. But this is still convenience, not the passionate, awesome, powerful, deeply connected love that is your primal yearning. More of your needs may be met—but your ultimate need will be unfulfilled. You might feel "happy," but not complete. You may eliminate some problems, but you won't feel connected and you won't recapture that special spark that once transformed your life.

A third option is to conclude that your spouse is not meeting your needs, get a divorce, and begin to search for someone new. Let me save you a lot of time, pain, and money—this probably won't work.

Statistically, your chances of divorcing the second time are higher than the first. Why? *Because your challenge is not to find the right person to love; it's to love the person you find.* This is important; let me explain.

Most people put very little effort into learning how to succeed in love, even though, as a society, we are failing in that endeavor, and love is what people want most. The reason is that most people think love depends on meeting the right person. You have to be "lucky in love," right? If the secret is to meet the right person—if it's luck that is needed—then why prepare? What is there to learn? No one prepares to play roulette, right?

If your goal is to find the right person, then your effort goes into that search—and into making yourself desirable so that when you find the right person, they want you. Ah, now there are two huge markets! The "get lucky in love" market which includes clubs, bars, gyms, and dating services, and the "look your best" market which includes fitness and diet programs, cosmetics, hair care, plastic surgery, fashion, jewelry, perfume, and automobiles. There is nothing wrong with meeting people or being fit and looking good, but those activities have nothing to do with building a strong marriage.

Most people spend more time, effort, and money trying to find the right person than they expend on learning to love the person that they waited for so long and looked so hard to find. But the emphasis should be reversed. Suppose your goal was to be a painter; would you spend most of your time learning how to paint or looking for the right model?

Love has very little to do with finding the right person. Most people who searched and chose the "right person" are now divorced. If you're asking whether or not you're with the right person, you might be asking the wrong question.

If you bought a Dell computer and couldn't figure out how to work it, would you throw it away so you could buy an IBM? If you don't know how to use a computer, changing brands isn't going to help.

The most important question is not how to find the right person—it's how to create and maintain a deep, loving connection with the person you find. Instead of searching for someone new, learn to love the one you're with.

If you want to be physically fit, you have to learn about diet and exercise and commit to a regular discipline. Marriage Fitness is like physical fitness—it's a skill that requires wisdom, practice, and commitment.

For most marriages, I suggest the fourth option: connect with your spouse and create phenomenal love in your marriage. You won't have nature on your side this time. You won't simply "fall in love." Building love is more like a climb. But with the MarriageMax™ 4-Step Plan, you can connect with your spouse again. And this time it doesn't have to be at the whim of nature. This time you can have control. You can "make love," and it doesn't have to end—ever.

Could things really be like they once were? Yes! Marriage Fitness is based on the universal laws of love. If you know and apply the laws, the results are predictable—you can "make" the connection. And when you do, you'll fall in love all over again.

Transforming Your Marriage

Why does connecting with your spouse change everything? Because love has transformative power.

Imagine yourself as a piece of a jigsaw puzzle with each protrusion and indentation representing a different aspect of your personality. Imagine your spouse has a puzzle piece with a unique pattern of protrusions and indentations too.

When you meet, there are points of compatibility and points of incompatibility. Sometimes your protrusions slide perfectly into your spouse's indentations. And sometimes things just don't fit. But one thing is for sure—the size and shape of your puzzle pieces (your personalities) don't change much throughout the years. If you're stubborn, the chances are good that you've always been stubborn.

Here are some interesting dynamics to consider. If your puzzle pieces (your personalities) don't change significantly, then why do you experience changes in your spouse and in your compatibility? If you and your spouse haven't changed much, then why did your love change?

How could you have been unaware of such obvious flaws in your spouse? Why did it take years for you to see things that everyone else knew on day one? How can so much change when so little changes?

There is a single answer to all these questions that offers piercing insight into how to create a phenomenal marriage.

Nothing really changes except love. But love changes your experience of everything. So when love changes, your experience of everything else changes too.

Your spouse and your compatibility don't change. The love in your marriage changes how you experience them. If you take away the golden lens, everything looks different.

Your spouse is not compassionate, for example. Your spouse has the capacity to be compassionate or harsh. The characteristic that you experience depends on your marriage. When you're in love, your spouse is compassionate. When you're not, your spouse is harsh. But what's causing the change is the state of your connection—your love.

You and your spouse have a third puzzle piece that fits between you. That puzzle piece is your love. Unlike the other two pieces, you can change this piece. You and your spouse create the love piece of your puzzle together. How you shape it determines how you fit. You and your spouse can be compatible or incompatible. You can be the most wonderful people in each other's lives or each other's enemies. It's all determined by the love piece of your puzzle. If you create love, you will be perfect for each other. If you don't, nothing will fit.

Your spouse and your compatibility don't change; your connection changes how you experience them! And by reconnecting, you can change your experience back.

You can't change anyone. To think you can change others is a huge mistake that many people make. When a marriage turns from sweet to sour, we tend to think it's the other person's fault. We think the other person changed and ruined everything. But people don't change much, and it wasn't a change in anyone that spoiled things. It's the loss of connection between a husband and wife—*that* spoils everything. As the old English proverb says, "Faults are thick where love is thin."

If you're lacking connection with your spouse, your experience of each other will be negatively impacted. If you reconnect, you'll regain the magic of your courtship. You can't change your spouse, but your connection can transform how you experience your spouse.

A person who falls in love is often asked, "What do you love about him?" Most people respond, "He brings out the best in me." The truth is—it's not *him* bringing out your best; it's the love. Love is the cause. Love determines your reality. It's the golden lens. Create love in your marriage and everything will be different.

Some people say "love is blind" but that implies that a person in love isn't seeing something. People who activate true, deep love are not blind to anything; they change everything. People in love see things differently not because they are blind, but because they are in love. For a person in love, things *are* different.

Cinderella asks, "Do you love me because I am beautiful, or am I beautiful because you love me?" The answer is— love is the great beautifier.

Sometimes people feel victim to a marriage they think their spouse caused to go sour. "He changed, and that's why we don't get along anymore. There's nothing I can do about it." In fact, the causality flows the other way. The marriage causes the change—not a person. And *that* you can do something about. You can transform your marriage. And your marriage will transform your experience of each other. The power lies within you. You are in control.

Couples sometimes make the mistake of changing aspects of their life that they think will make them happy. My wife and I were sure that selling our house and moving to a different community would make a big difference in our lives. But usually changes like that don't impact anything beyond the thing itself. Love, on the other hand, impacts everything. It's the heart that pumps blood to every limb.

This is why focusing on communication skills and problem-solving, while helpful, miss the target. It's not the root issue. It's not the heart of the matter. It merely treats the symptom. You could master both skills and still be completely unfulfilled in your marriage and without true love in your life. Whereas, if you address the root of your marriage, and consummate a connection with your spouse, you will experience euphoric love and your problems will fade away. *Love conquers all. It is the root of transformation.*

Summary

Love is the most awesome experience in life because it fulfills our most basic need—the need to connect with another person. But falling in love is a gift from Mother Nature which doesn't last forever. When ecstatic love fades from your relationship, so does the ecstasy from your life. You also experience flaws in your spouse and incompatibilities in your relationship. But neither your spouse nor your compatibility changed. Your love changed, and that changed your experience of everything.

At this point in your marriage, you have four options.

1. Lower your expectations and navigate a marriage that "works." If you select this option, your experience could vary from dissatisfaction to happiness, but you

will not achieve true love or ultimate fulfillment in life.

2. Improve your marriage by focusing on some of your marital issues. This approach may enhance your marriage, but once again, you will miss out on true love and ultimate fulfillment.

3. Divorce or separate and seek love in another relationship. This won't work because the key to a successful marriage is not finding the right person; it's learning to love the person you found.

4. Reconnect with your spouse. You connected when you fell in love. You can do it again. The first time was a gift. This time you'll have to "make" love. You can do it, and MARRIAGE FITNESS shows you how.

When you "make" love—when you reconnect—everything changes "from frog to prince." Love is a golden lens through which your spouse and your life look wonderful. Love quenches your deepest desire and it is there that you will find ultimate fulfillment in your marriage and in your life.

Chapter 2

HOW TO FIND THE SOUL OF YOUR MATE

Creating love between you and your spouse is the key to a phenomenal marriage and a fulfilling life. But in order to understand the depth of that idea, you have to know what I mean when I say "love." What *really* is love? And what *really* is the connection that is the secret to creating it?

Love is *not* a mystery! Love is actually quite simple. But in order to appreciate love's simplicity, we have to explore some complex issues.

The former Supreme Court Justice Oliver Wendell Holmes said, "I would not give a fig for the simplicity this side of complexity, but I would give my life for the simplicity on the other side of complexity." In other words, the most difficult questions usually have simple answers, but you can't understand how profound the simple answer is unless you struggle with the complexity of the question. For example, you can't get any simpler than $E=mc^2$, but there are very few people with enough knowledge of physics who are able to grasp the brilliance of Einstein's discovery.

Love is simple, but you can only appreciate its simplicity after you go through its complexities. Follow closely the discussion in this chapter, and soon you will appreciate the simple truth about love.

Knowing Your Spouse

Connecting is the key to creating love. But in order to connect with your spouse, you need to know where in your marriage to create that connection. What part of you, when connected with the corresponding part of your spouse, is transformative? In other words, where does love happen?

One night, my wife and I invited some friends to dinner. One friend asked why I sold my business and traveled around the world for a year. I explained that I wanted to embark on a journey of self-discovery. I wanted to take time to "find myself."

Just as I made that remark, my son, who was three-years-old at the time, looked at me inquisitively. I could see from the expression on his face that he was confused. "What does it mean that Daddy took time to find himself?" he probably wondered. "How did he lose himself in the first place?"

Our dinner guests seemed to understand what I meant, but I wonder if it would have been more honest of them to be confused like my son.

What does it mean to find yourself? Who are *you*? What was I looking for on my journey of self-discovery? Why would I travel around the world to find myself? No matter where I go, isn't that where I am? If I had "found" myself, what would I have discovered? Who am *I,* really?

When someone meets you for the first time, they might ask you, "What's your name? Where are you from? What do you do?" They're asking these questions in order to get to know you. Your appearance and manners offer them information too. A business suit makes a different personal statement than a T-shirt. Eventually, people also get to know your qualities—whether you are warm or aloof, friendly or reserved, rude or gracious, angry or good-natured, charming or boorish, obnoxious or agreeable, kind or mean-spirited.

Think about yourself. What are you like? If you were in a movie, how would you describe your character? What is your scene? What is your role? Take some time to consider your appearance, your health, your physique, your social life, your family life, your work life, your finances, your personality, your abilities, your disposition, your environment, and your outlook on life. Using these categories as a guide, make a list of everything you know about yourself.

Review your list. Do you like yourself? Identify something on your list you want to change and with it in mind say, "I want to change myself." What did you mean when you said that? Who is the *I* that wants to change, and who is the *self* that would be changed? Think about that question for a moment before you read on.

When you say you like yourself, hate yourself, or want to change yourself, you make *yourself* both the subject and the object of the same sentence. How can that be?

When you say, "I like myself," who is the *I* doing the liking? Who is the *self* being liked? What is the distinction between *I* and *myself*—between the subject and the object?

On the one hand, there is no distinction. *I* am one person. On the other hand, the way we speak reflects that we intuit a distinction and a multiplicity within our sole being. And this is precisely the confusion my son experienced when I said I was looking for myself.

There is only one you, but there is duality within you. "Who am I?" is not a simple question to answer. The poet Walt Whitman said, "I am vast. I contain multitudes."

Let's further explore the duality within you because understanding it is essential to connecting with your spouse and creating true love.

There are two aspects to your existence. First, there is your character, which is everything you know about yourself. It's critical to understand that when I refer to your "character," I mean much more than just your character traits. Your character is the entire role you play in life. It's everything on the list you made describing yourself. It's everything and anything you could say about yourself. Your character includes your character traits, but like a character in a movie, your character also includes your appearance, your health, your physique, your social life, your family life, your work life, your finances, your personality, your abilities, your disposition, your environment, and your outlook on life.

My character is named Mort Fertel. He's five foot ten inches tall and 145 pounds. He has brown hair and blue eyes and he often wears a navy-blue cardigan sweater. He lives in Baltimore with his wife and four children. He is an author, businessman, and Marriage Fitness coach. He likes to read, write, and be with his family. He does not like to cook or do house repairs. His strengths are… His weaknesses are… He believes… He does not believe… All these types of things are part of our character.

The second aspect to your existence is more difficult to describe and understand. You can't say anything about it. It's that part of you *not* on your list. It's not on your list because it's the part of you that made the list. In other words, there's your character, which is everything about you that can be observed (your list), and then there's the observer within you. Another way to look at this is to look at the difference between everything about yourself that you like and dislike, and the *you* that is formulating those preferences. There is a part of you that you know, and then there is a part of you that knows. This part of you is uniquely human. It's what allows you to be self-aware.

Do you ever get angry with yourself? How does that work? Who's angry with whom? Did you ever talk to yourself? Who's talking to whom? Did you ever make yourself laugh? Who's laughing at whom? Do you see that there is another part of you that interacts with your character?

When you were a child, did you ever ask yourself who you would be if your mother had married another man? That's a strange question, isn't it? It's a profound question too, because children who ask that question intuit the duality of their nature. A child who asks, "Who would *I* be if my mother had married another man?" senses that the part of himself that is self-aware, his *I,* his knower, could be matched with a completely different character. The new character could look different, have different parents, live in a different place, and play with different toys. Everything the child knows about himself could be different—he could be a completely different character—but the question the child asks is still "who would *I* be if my mother had married another man?" because the child intuits that in the most essential way, he would still be himself—the same knower, the same *I.* The child knows that his character can change, but his *I,* the self-aware part of himself, cannot.

Think about how much you've changed over the years. You can easily see some of these changes in your photo album. Think through the stages of your life and what you were like during them. Think about a time in your life when you were very different from the way you are now. Recall your appearance, your health, your physique, your social life, your family life, your work life, your finances, your abilities, your environment, and your outlook on life. (Recall your personality and disposition which are part of your character too. They may have changed, but as explained in Chapter 1, they usually do not). Make another list describing yourself during this stage of your life.

Compare this list with the list you made earlier in the chapter. Notice how much you've changed. Now, consider that you are the same. You've changed, but *you* were always you, right? It's the same knower knowing a new character. One part of you changed, but another part of you is constant.

The duality of your existence is evident even at the molecular level. Biologists explain that every day cells of your body die and are replaced with new ones until eventually you are, physically, not the same person. And yet, you know there is a part of you that is exactly the same. Physically, your character is constantly changing. Essentially, *you* remain the same.

Think about your compact disc player. The music you

hear changes depending on the compact disc you insert. But regardless of the music being played, it's always the same player.

Your character changes over time like compact discs in a player. However, there is a part of you—your knower, your essential *I*—that never changes. It's like the compact disc player. It experiences the changes but remains constant. It's fixed while the other part of you is in flux.

Without getting too mystical, the part of you that is aware of your changing character is your soul. Your soul is your core—your essential self. Your soul observes all the changes in your life while remaining constant. It's the compact disc player. It's your unchanging *I*.

How does this relate to connecting with your spouse and creating phenomenal love in your marriage?

The Duality of Your Existence	
1	**2**
Soul	Role
Core	Character
Fixed	Flux
Knower	Known
List Maker	List
Unchanging *I*	Changing You
Compact Disc Player	Compact Discs

Becoming Soul Mates

To create phenomenal love in your marriage, you have to connect with your spouse. But what do you connect? Do you connect your characters or your souls?

If you try to connect your characters, you're "looking for love in all the wrong places." You may have the best intentions. You and your spouse may put forth a valiant effort. You may learn to get along better and fight less. But connecting your characters so they are compatible will not create love in your marriage or fulfillment in your life. Love is a result of a core connection. That's what it means to be soul mates.

Compatibility is a worthy objective for friends, acquaintances, and business associates. It's important to learn how to get along with people. It's even important to extend a special effort to improve your compatibility with certain people such as your family, your boss, or your office colleagues. But compatibility is not the objective of marriage, and it certainly doesn't lead to profound love.

Imagine walking in New York City and someone in their car rolls down their window and asks, "Excuse me, but could you tell me how to get to the London Bridge?"

Sometimes we're in the wrong place asking the wrong question. If you're in a car in New York City, you can't get to the London Bridge. And if you're focused on compatibility, you can't get to transformative love.

Most of us were raised with a Calvinist work ethic and taught that we can accomplish anything if we try hard enough. But success in some things is not a function of effort. Sometimes it's a matter of wisdom. If you're driving in New York City, it doesn't matter how hard you try to get to the London Bridge, you won't get there. But with a little wisdom, you could make your way to the airport and be at the London Bridge within twenty-four hours.

Everyone wants a phenomenal marriage. But most couple's efforts for love are actually efforts for greater compatibility. But improving compatibility to find love is like driving in New York City looking for the London Bridge. You won't find it. You're in the wrong place.

I remember trying desperately to solve our marital problems. My wife and I were very frustrated with each other. The harder we tried, the more stressed-out we felt. Every time we talked about a problem, not only did we fail to resolve it, but we ended up fighting too. Our efforts to make things better kept making matters worse.

The turning point for us was when we shifted our focus from improving compatibility to connecting at our cores. When we stopped dealing with our problems and started becoming soul mates, that's when we found solutions.

Creating phenomenal love is a process of becoming soul mates. It has very little to do with character compatibility.

Success in love takes more than work—it takes wisdom. You have to know where to direct your efforts. Transformative love occurs at your core. Direct your efforts there.

How to Endure Change

When you and your spouse connect at your cores and become soul mates, you experience life very differently than if your marriage is based on compatibility. Let's explore some significant ways life can be different for you.

In Chapter 1, we discussed that you and your spouse's personality do not change significantly. However, there are many aspects of your character that *do* change. Your bodies change. Your careers are likely to change. You enjoy different hobbies at different stages of your life. Most of your character is in constant flux.

If your marriage is based on compatibility, you and your spouse's character changes will upset your relationship. Consider a man who divorces his wife primarily because she became a career woman instead of the homemaker he married. He didn't want his wife to change, but divorcing her is like returning a compact disc player because he didn't like the music it played. Characters change. That's a fact of life. If your marriage is based on compatibility, you're on shaky ground.

Soul mates, on the other hand, flow with each other's character changes because their marriage is not dependent upon their compatibility. Soul mates have a core connection that transcends their characters. Individually, soul mates change like everyone. But their marriage is insulated from those changes. It's secure at the core.

Marriages based on compatibility can be threatened by character changes. If you're satisfied in your marriage because of the extravagant lifestyle your spouse provides, then your marriage could be threatened if your spouse's business went bankrupt or the stock market crashed. If you're satisfied in your marriage because your spouse is a good care-taker, then your marriage might be threatened if your spouse was stricken with a debilitating illness. If you're satisfied in your marriage because of your spouse's appearance, then your marriage may experience stress as your spouse ages.

Most couples try to solve the problems that character changes create. For example, if one spouse is becoming more religious, the other may agree to attend services once a week. Just as some character changes strain marriage, others can provide relief. Like a scientist trying to find the right chemical balance, a couple can make adjustments in an effort to maintain equilibrium. Efforts like these are not completely futile, and character compatibility is certainly not bad. However, these efforts do not create love. They create compatibility. And the two are as far part as London and New York.

Marriages based on character compatibility are tenuous. You never know when your spouse will add a chemical that will disrupt the equilibrium. What if you change and your spouse cannot adjust? What if something beyond everyone's control changes the mix? Change is the enemy of marriages based on compatibility. Since change is a constant in life, marriages based on compatibility have a lot of battles to fight.

If you're in a marriage based on compatibility, you're sitting on a time-bomb. Eventually some change will threaten your compatibility and trigger conflict. You can problem-solve, but that will only provide relief until the next change. If your marriage is based on compatibility, it's vulnerable and so are you.

Consider a comic strip depicting a man trying desperately to get out of a box. He tries to climb over the top and

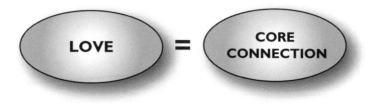

cut through the walls. Finally, he escapes the box. In the next frame, the man is sitting outside the box wiping his brow and breathing a sigh of relief. "Thank God I got out of that box," he says. But the reader can see something he cannot, which is that he is trapped inside another box.

The problem with a marriage based on compatibility is that no matter how hard you try, no matter how many problems you solve, you're always trapped in a box. There's always a problem to solve or one that lays dormant. The only way out is to shift the focus of your marriage from your characters to your cores. The only way out is to become soul mates.

Unfortunately, true love eludes most people not because they don't find Mr. or Mrs. Right, but because they connect with them in the wrong place. *True love is not about compatibility; it's about making a core connection.*

Consider your marriage. Is it based mostly on compatibility? Is your marriage dependent upon you or your spouse's looks, money, opinions, attitudes, social manner, travel interests, hobbies, career, or wardrobe?

The key to achieving phenomenal love is not the ability to navigate the complexities of your marriage; rather, it's the ability to realize the simplicity of it. The challenge is to see past the externalities to the soul of the matter. This is where love happens, and this is where a marriage is protected from change. Connect at your cores, and you can change careers, hairstyles, hobbies, interests, friends, favorite restaurants, and fashion preferences. Through all your changes, your love will last.

Unfortunately, there are heartbreaking stories about marriages breaking up after life-changing illnesses, face-maiming accidents, and bankruptcies. These are terrible challenges that can forever alter your life, but love can endure. *Connect at your core and your marriage can survive anything.*

My wife and I are blessed with four healthy children, but our road to conceiving a family was extremely difficult. During her pregnancies, my wife spent many months in the hospital and on bed rest at home. When my wife was pregnant with triplets, I was home alone for four months with our three-year-old, while my wife was confined to bed rest in the hospital. This was a very challenging time in our life. For practical purposes, I was a single father caring for a three-year-old, while running back and forth to the hospital to see my wife and trying to uphold my responsibilities at work.

As difficult as that pregnancy was, it doesn't compare to the trauma that we experienced on two separate pregnancies when my wife gave birth to children who died in the hospital less than one week after their birth.

You never know what life will bring, but soul mates know they can always rely on each other. Change can be all around you—the drama of life surrounding you—but stability and peace can be between you. Not even death will do you part. Soul mates are forever.

William Shakespeare wrote:

> *Let me not to the marriage of true minds*
> *Admit impediments. Love is not love*
> *Which alters when it alteration finds,*
> *Or bends with the remover to remove.*
> *O no! it is an ever-fixed mark*
> *That looks on tempests and is never shaken;*
> *It is the star to every wand'ring bark,*
> *Whose worth's unknown, although his height be taken.*
> *Love's not Time's fool, though rosy lips and cheeks*
> *Within his bending sickle's compass come.*
> *Love alters not with his brief hours and weeks,*
> *But bears it out even to the edge of doom.*

If this be error, and upon me proved,
I never writ, nor no man ever loved.

Connect at your core. From there you can endure.

The Freedom to be Yourself

Do you hide things from your spouse? Do you feel inhibited? Are you hesitant to *really* be yourself?

If you answered "yes," you have a symptom of a marriage based on compatibility. You're hesitant to be yourself because you feel that your spouse won't love you. But the part of yourself you're scared won't be loved is not *you;* it's your character. Your fear is legitimate only if your marriage is based on your characters and not on your core.

Soul mates can be themselves. When two people connect at their cores, they experience love regardless of their characters. It's not that soul mates don't have addictions, haunted pasts, body image issues, and other problems. Soul mates have flaws just like everyone else. The difference is—soul mates don't hide them. They don't have to. Their marriage is not dependent upon them being any particular character.

Usually, the more impressive a person appears, the more we love them. So people appear as impressive as possible. But that's the experience of *role mates.* Soul mates have a different experience.

Soul mates are natural with each other. They're not trying to impress each other. In fact, the deeper a couple's core connection, the freer they are to be themselves and the less impressive they may appear to each other. For soul mates, appearances of character flaws are mitigated by the fact that their marriage is not based on their characters. True love actually exposes the most, but what's exposed ends up meaning the least.

My wife and I once asked each other to share one thing about ourselves that we wouldn't want anyone else to know. I realize now that we each had a long list from which to choose. But as our love grew, so did our willingness to share.

Now we know the most, but it means the least. It's our love that matters.

"What do you love about him/her?" your friend asks when you're falling in love. "I love that I can just be myself," you respond. But why do you feel you can be yourself? It's because you connected at your cores. When you're soul mates, you can be any character. But if you're role mates, you're stuck with who you are.

Escaping Judgment

Do you feel inadequate with your spouse? Do you feel superior? Do you feel judged by your spouse? Do you judge?

Once again, if you answered "yes," you have a symptom of a marriage based on compatibility. Judgment and feelings of inadequacy or superiority result from character comparisons. But when the focus of your marriage is a core connection, there's nothing to measure. Every soul is incomparable.

Some people trade-in their marriages like they trade-in cars. As one starts to wear down in their eyes, they shop for an improved model. Many people go through five to ten significant relationships in their lifetime, including two or three marriages. In the beginning of each relationship, it seems they found a better deal. However, in time, each model wears down in their eyes and history reveals a string of relationships with people whose characters are similar. But the problem is never the model. The problem is that they judge their spouse's character instead of connecting with their spouse's core.

How many times have we heard stories of someone leaving their spouse for another mate? There are usually numerous reasons why people do this, but one of them is that people look for the newest and the best of everything. There is always someone with more hair, more money, more compassion, fewer problems, a better body, more muscles, and more energy. There's always a better deal out there is the perspective of someone looking for a role mate, not a soul mate. *But role mates never last. Soul mates are forever.*

Don't judge or compare. In your quest for the best, you'll fail to win the most important prize—love. At your cores, you can have it all—and nothing compares.

Getting Great Advice

Soul mates don't judge, but they do critique. In fact, soul mates are each other's best critics. When you connect at your cores, you find your soul mate and you find your life coach too.

Soul mates *can* be any character, but they *want* each other to be their best character. Soul mates don't coach each other because they need their spouse to change. Soul mates only need love. Love comes from the core, not from character improvement. But soul mates *want* each other to improve their characters because they want the best for each other. Their coaching is an expression of love, not selfishness. When you love someone, you want what's best for them.

A friend once critiqued a business practice of mine. He had no way to benefit from my business improving. He was completely objective—and it was his objectivity that made him an effective and credible coach. If he had something to gain, he wouldn't be able to give objective advice and I wouldn't have been able to trust him.

To be a good coach, you can't have an agenda. You can only have one interest—your spouse.

If I advise my wife to exercise regularly because I'm attracted to athletic women, I'm being her role mate, not her soul mate. I'm not coaching; I'm judging. In order for me to be my wife's soul mate and her coach, I can only have one reason for wanting her to be physically fit—because it's good for her! Any other reason will sour the advice and soil our marriage.

Soul mates are good coaches for each other because their marriage is not based on their characters. Soul mates don't need each other to improve for love. They *want* each other to improve *because* of their love.

Finding Security in Your Marriage

There is no worse feeling than being in a marriage with someone you think could leave you. We want to feel safe. We want to be with someone who is committed—no matter what. But many people feel vulnerable—even after marrying. Many people sense that their spouse's commitment is conditional.

People impose all sorts of conditions on their spouses. Men are notorious for making their love dependent upon a certain frequency of sexual activity. A person might be committed to the marriage as long as there is not too much fighting. Conditional marriages, including ones in which the conditions are met consistently, are inherently insecure because there is no certainty that any condition can be met forever.

Do you feel secure in your marriage? Is your marriage conditional? Who is imposing the conditions and what are they?

You cannot achieve security in your marriage by trying to secure your conditions. Security comes from dropping your conditions and connecting at your cores.

At your core, there is a permanent root of love no matter what—sickness or health, poverty or wealth, trauma or peace. There are no conditions. At your core, love is secure. And I'm not talking about the security that comes from a promise or a vow. I'm talking about a deep security that is beyond words—a safety that can only be known by your soul.

A friend of mine once told me why his fiancé was perfect for him. He explained his love for her in great detail. I was amazed he had so many reasons why they were right for each other. I knew it was a mistake. I knew she wasn't right. My friend spoke of conditions. But true love is ineffable. Soul mates are speechless.

Soul mates don't have reasons for feeling secure in their marriage. The reason for their security is that they are soul mates.

When spouses focus on conditions, they're not soul mates; they're role mates. But roles change, which is why marriages anchored in compatibility are not safe. Only soul mates are forever.

Summary

There are two aspects to your existence.

1. Your character, which is the role you play in life. Your character is everything you know about yourself including your character traits, personality, appearance, health, career, physique, social life, family life, finances, abilities, disposition, and your outlook on life.

2. Your soul. This is your essential self—the core of your existence.

Your character changes over time like compact discs in a player. However, your soul never changes. It's like the compact disc player that plays different music. It experiences the changes of your character but remains constant. It's fixed while your character is in flux.

This distinction is crucial because in order to make the connection with your spouse that transforms your marriage and your life, you have to know what to connect. Character compatibility is nice, but it has very little to do with true love. On the other hand, when you and your spouse become soul mates—when you connect at the core of your existence—the golden lens appears and your marriage and your life are transformed forever. This is the experience of love.

Connecting at your core and creating love in your marriage has some distinctive advantages over a marriage based on compatibility. Those advantages are:

1. Your characters can change without those changes upsetting your marriage.

2. You and your spouse are completely free to be yourselves.

3. You and your spouse won't judge each other or be judged by each other.

4. You and your spouse will become each other's best advisor and most trusted life coach.

5. You will experience true security in your marriage.

We've arrived at the million dollar question. How do you and your spouse become soul mates? How do you create that core connection which results in phenomenal love and ultimate fulfillment in life? The answer is the MarriageMax™ 4-Step Plan.

PART II:

THE MARRIAGEMAX™ 4-STEP PLAN

Chapter 3

LOVE IS A VERB

Fine restaurants often serve intermezzo between courses. It's usually a small dish of flavored ice that's intended to cleanse your palate before the next course. On the menu, it counts as a separate course, but its primary purpose is transitional.

This chapter is like intermezzo. It's small and it has its own flavor, but its primary purpose is transitional.

At this point we have discussed what is essential to know about love. In short, love changes your experience of everything. And love is not compatibility; it's a soul connection. The coming chapters of MARRIAGE FITNESS discuss how to create love—how to become soul mates with your spouse.

Climbing in Love

Love is not a feeling—it's something you do. You make a decision to love, and then you act. It's a choice and a deed. Love is a verb.

Chapters 4 through 7 present the MarriageMax™ 4-Step Plan. Within the four steps are twenty exercises. The MarriageMax™ 4-Step Plan teaches you how to "make love" with your clothes on.

It's not difficult to "make love." You can implement these four steps immediately and create phenomenal love within weeks. It's definitely not rocket science. However, it does require effort, time, and commitment. You can't just sit there and expect the fireworks to go off in the background.

Marriage Fitness is not a quick fix. Marriage Fitness addresses the root of your relationship. To affect the root, you have to role up your sleeves, dig down, and cultivate consistently. It takes work. It takes effort. It takes time. But the result is not simply the solution to problems or a compatible marriage; it's the transformation of your relationship.

A physical fitness program takes more effort than liposuction, but the results are authentic and longer lasting. Marriage Fitness takes discipline just like physical fitness, but the outcome is a fundamental transformation of your marriage, not merely a symptomatic one.

Nothing truly worthwhile is easy. Marriage Fitness is no exception. But if you commit to the discipline of the MarriageMax™ 4-Step Plan, both the process and the results will be rewarding and profound.

Are you ready? Are you willing to do the work?

You might be thinking, "If my marriage takes so much work and time, then something must be wrong—I must be with the wrong person." But the key to love is not finding the right person; it's learning to build lasting love with the person you found. And that's not easy. Hollywood portrays love as easy, but that's only in the movies, not in real life. Love was easy during your courtship, but that was when you had Mother Nature on your side. After a couple of years, those batteries are dead. Mother Nature leaves it up to you to keep your marriage charged. You're not going to fall in love again—at least not with the same person. You're going to have to "make love." It's going to take time and effort.

Think about it for a moment—you understand that this is how life works. You get out of something what you put into it. No pain, no gain, right? In every other aspect of life you understand that success takes commitment, time, effort, and hard work. Why would you expect the most important thing in life, love—the one thing that transforms all else in life—to be any different?

What if you don't feel like loving? What if you're angry or bitter? Love anyway. The best way to change how you feel is to change what you do. If you start loving you will start feeling different. If you wait until you feel different, you'll be stuck forever.

I want to offer a word of caution. If you're not used to devoting significant time and energy to your marriage, the MarriageMax™ 4-Step Plan can be overwhelming at first. There's no need to be overwhelmed. You don't have to implement everything at once. In fact, you should *not* implement everything at once.

A Marriage Fitness plan is like a physical fitness plan— you can't go from zero to Olympic-level over the weekend. It takes time, patience, and discipline. At the conclusion of this book, there is a section about the importance of implementing the plan at a reasonable pace and being comfortable with the exercises you've adopted before increasing your Marriage Fitness plan. There is also a suggested fourteen-week schedule for implementation. It's important to go slow. There's no rush and no reason to feel overwhelmed.

Here is the MarriageMax™ 4-Step Plan. Let's get to work.

The MarriageMax™ 4-Step Plan

1. **Put Love First**
2. Give Presence
3. Move from Me to We
4. Save Yourself

Chapter 4

PUT LOVE FIRST

Millard Fuller was a small town boy from modest means. He aspired to grand financial success and high status in the business community. He married his wife, Linda, when they were young. Although they struggled to make ends meet, they were happy.

Millard worked hard in pursuit of his financial dream and became a millionaire when he was only twenty-nine years old.

The Fullers had it all—homes, cars, clothes, expensive vacations, jewelry, power, influence, security… whatever money could buy. However, as is often the case with success stories like this, the more Millard immersed himself in his business, the more he neglected his wife. Millard's marriage, which began as a passionate love affair, became his "side business." His bank account grew by leaps and bounds, but his marriage account depleted just as quickly.

Linda became frustrated with their marriage and began a silent protest. Millard's mind was at work even when his body was home. He missed all the signs of Linda's quiet misery and continued to immerse himself in his business. Eventually, the situation became unbearable for Linda.

One day Linda visited Millard at his office and announced, "I don't think I love you anymore." Millard couldn't believe what he heard. Linda explained that he gave her everything she wanted except what she wanted most—a husband. She wanted him, but he was unavailable.

Millard promised Linda he would change. But one year later, he had not. Linda's patience was exhausted. She was completely disenchanted. Finally, Linda left Millard and traveled to New York.

With Linda gone, Milliard felt helpless. For the first time in his life, he was not in control. Millard's business was thriving, but his life was crashing.

While Linda was in New York, Millard was forced to care for their children—a rarity in the Fuller home. One night, while he was tucking his son into bed, his son gazed into his eyes and said, "Daddy, I'm glad you're here." There was something about his son's simple but genuine comment that opened Millard's eyes—and the truth about himself filled his heart. He had neglected his family.

Millard flew to New York as soon as possible to see his wife. Linda unloaded years of heartbreak. Her silent misery erupted into a long angry monologue. Millard listened. They reflected on the rise of his business and the fall of their marriage. Millard shared with Linda the disappointment he felt in himself—devastated that he had failed her. Then Millard made a life changing decision. He chose to put love first.

Millard sold everything and gave away most of his money (he founded Habitat for Humanity). He cleansed his life of anything that prevented him from focusing on his marriage. He moved his family into a modest home, where he and Linda began to rebuild their marriage.

Millard Fuller gave up everything for his wife and his marriage. He decided that their love would be the most important thing in the world to him because he realized that it *is* the most important thing in the world.

Millard achieved great success, but without love in his life, he was bankrupt—and he knew it. Millard understood that if he didn't make love the highest priority in his life—if he didn't succeed in his marriage—then he would fail in his life. It's true, and so is his story.

There are millions of people who, individually, achieve their dreams, but whose love life is a nightmare. Since love conquers all—since *it* is the dominant force—it determines the experience of your life. Therefore, love should come first. It should be your top priority.

Your love life can transform how you experience every other aspect of your life. But no other aspect of your life—no matter how good it is—can compensate for lack of love in your marriage.

When you're in love, work is fantastic, you look good, you feel energetic and you always have enough money—life is great. But if you're not connected at the core with your spouse—if you're not in love—everything is a problem.

An ancient tradition teaches that two people in love can sleep on the edge of a razor blade. But if there is not love between them, no bed will be big enough. Love *is* the answer. *When you have love in your life, nothing else matters. If you don't have it, nothing else will be enough.*

Put love first in your life. Make it your top priority.

How important is your marriage in your life? Does your spouse have your heart or is it invested elsewhere? Is your marriage your top priority or do you sometimes give something else the right of way?

Step one of the MarriageMax™ 4-Step Plan for connecting your cores and building phenomenal love is to make your spouse and your marriage the absolute highest priority in your life bar none. In other words—step one is to *put love first.*

Just as Millard Fuller became attached to his business when it was his priority, he connected with his wife when she became his priority. *Whatever is important to you is what connects with you. Prioritize your spouse and you'll have a soul mate. Prioritize something else and you'll be married to it.*

The Only Change You Need to Make

Fortunately, you don't have to liquidate everything in order for your spouse and your marriage to be your top priority. In

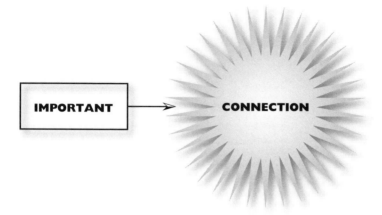

fact, you don't have to liquidate anything. The point of the Millard Fuller story is not how much Millard was willing to change, but how much he was willing to change his focus. Your priority is the crucial factor.

Millard's wife could have been his top priority without him selling anything (imagine, he could have had it all—love and riches). To transform his marriage, Millard didn't have to turn his whole life upside down. He simply had to change his priorities. He didn't have to leave his business; he simply had to make his marriage more important than his business.

What liberating news! Some people are scared to try to improve their marriage because they think it means that they will have to make dramatic changes in their life. It's not necessarily true. The secret is not simply change; it's change of priority.

You can change something about yourself in order to get along better with your spouse. That's certainly not a crime, and your spouse won't complain. But the fact that you get along better does not mean that you will experience true love. Changing can help you get along better. Changing your priority—that will connect your cores and transform your life.

Maybe you're wondering if it's possible for you or your spouse to change enough to really please each other. But that's not the critical question. The question is not whether you are willing to change. The question is whether you're willing to change your priorities. Changing won't change much. Changing your priority can change everything.

If you're worried about what you might have to change to improve your marriage, let those worries go. If you're waiting for your spouse to change so that your marriage will change, relieve yourself of that anticipation. If you're pressuring your spouse to change, take the pressure off. Instead, decide now that your spouse is the highest priority in your life and begin immediately to behave in ways that reflect that priority. That's the only change you need to make.

Prioritizing

When your spouse calls you at work or on your cell phone, do you talk, or do you call back because whatever or whoever you're involved with takes priority? Consider the opposite scenario. If you're with your spouse and the phone rings, do you talk, or do you call back because your spouse takes priority?

Do you have any weekly activities to which you are committed? A card game? A tennis match? A music lesson? Bowling night? Guys/girls night out? An exercise class? A board meeting? A TV show? Religious services? A study group? I'm not suggesting that these activities shouldn't be part of your weekly routine. But let me ask you this—do you have scheduled time with your spouse each week? Do you have committed time set aside for each other?

What does your lifestyle say about what you value most? How do you choose to spend your time and energy?

If you told your spouse that you would be home by a certain time, is your commitment to your spouse most important? Or is it more important to make one more phone call, write one more email, play one more round, run one more lap, finish your meal, or spend a few more minutes with your friend?

Countless opportunities present themselves every day to proclaim your priority. Review your typical day, week, month, and year. Consider how you can increase the importance that

Put Love First Marriage Assessment

If you began a physical fitness program, you would first want to establish your "baseline"—a measure of where you are now. A good assessment helps you focus on the areas that need the most attention and allows you to track your overall progress. Marriage Fitness is no different.

The following assessment measures the degree of importance you give to your marriage. Answer the questions below "true" or "false." Compare your score with the assessment scale below. Take the test periodically after you begin your Marriage Fitness program to monitor your progress.

		True	False
1.	When my spouse phones, I almost always make time to talk.	☐	☐
2.	If I'm with my spouse and someone else phones, I usually don't take the call.	☐	☐
3.	I speak to my spouse about non-logistical matters at least twice per day.	☐	☐
4.	When something significant happens in my life, I almost always share it with my spouse first.	☐	☐
5.	I initiate positive loving physical contact with my spouse at least twice each day.	☐	☐
6.	When we go to a social function, I almost always spend at least half my time talking with my spouse.	☐	☐
7.	When my spouse walks into the house, I almost always interrupt whatever I am doing to greet my spouse.	☐	☐
8.	When I walk into the house, the first thing I usually do is greet my spouse.	☐	☐
9.	I spend more time interacting with my spouse than I do watching TV.	☐	☐
10.	I spend more time interacting with my spouse than anyone else in my life.	☐	☐

	True	False
11. I usually interrupt whatever I am doing if my spouse wants my attention.	☐	☐
12. When I need someone to talk to, I almost always talk to my spouse.	☐	☐
13. I almost always recognize in a significant way my spouse's birthday, our anniversary, and other special days.	☐	☐
14. My spouse and I go out alone together at least once per week.	☐	☐
15. My spouse and I go on vacation alone together at least once per year.	☐	☐
16. I have photographs of my spouse in my office, wallet, or gym locker.	☐	☐
17. I have at least one personal and meaningful discussion with my spouse per week for a minimum of twenty-five minutes.	☐	☐
18. I do unnecessary thoughtful things for my spouse regularly.	☐	☐

Add the number of times you answered "true" and write your score here ☐

Rate your score.

1–8: OUT OF SHAPE. You need to work hard to increase the importance you give to your spouse and your marriage. The above questions may indicate some areas you should concentrate on.

9–13: AVERAGE. But don't settle for average. Your marriage is the most important thing in your life. It should be great! Try to *put love first* more often.

14-18: MARRIAGE FITNESS CHAMPION. You seem to have your priorities straight. What else could you do to give your marriage even higher priority?

your spouse and your marriage has in your life. Ask your spouse for suggestions and try to implement them into your lifestyle.

When you ask your assistant to hold all calls, does she know to make an exception for your spouse? If you're in a meeting and are told that your spouse is on the phone, will you take the call, no matter what? Would you take the call if your boss was on the phone, no matter what?

If you want to be healthy, you have to make exercise and diet a priority in your life. You have to be conscious of your caloric intake and think about the types of foods you eat. You have to plan an exercise routine and commit time to it. In short, you have to make your health a priority in your life. It takes time, thought, energy, and commitment. The same applies to your marriage. If you want to succeed in love, it has to be a priority in your life. And since love is where success matters most, your marriage should be your top priority.

Giving and Getting Attention

To *put love first* requires time and focus. There are no short-cuts. There is no microwave version. There's no high-speed route. You can't give someone else power of attorney. You have to do it the old-fashioned way. You have to pay attention.

I sometimes take my son camping. It intensifies our relationship. One of the benefits of camping is that there are no distractions. We're in the middle of nowhere with nothing to do except build a fire, pitch the tent, and be together. When my son calls my name or tries to get my attention, there's no competition. I'm there for him 100 percent. It's a bonding experience.

You probably can't live in a campground with your spouse and be responsible for only building fires and pitching tents. But you can learn to focus more on your spouse and you can learn to prioritize better.

You probably have the best opportunity to connect with your spouse in the evenings and on weekends. What happens in your house in the evening? Do you and your spouse tune into the TV or pay attention to each other?

If you're watching a program or reading a magazine and your spouse wants to talk to you, how do you respond? Do you make your spouse wait or does your spouse get your immediate attention?

Unfortunately, most couples don't talk to each other much anymore. Most couples spend more time facing the TV than they spend facing each other. Turn the TV off! Face each other. Put the magazine down. Read your spouse's expression. Get off the phone with your friend. Talk to your spouse. Log off the web and connect with each other. Pay attention to what is most important. Prioritize your marriage above everything else.

Being a good spouse is not about any one Herculean event. It's not enough to be there for your spouse in crisis. Marriage is about being there for your spouse thousands of times, day in and day out, for years. It's about a short chat on the phone, leaving a love note, doing a favor, helping out for no reason, bringing home a small gift, picking up the dry cleaning, asking the right question—it's about paying attention and focus. *Good spouses do small things in great ways.*

If you don't *put love first,* you will not be fulfilled. You could be busy with shopping, working, lunch dates, carpool, evening activities, exercise, social events, and TV programs—everything could be in order, the house could look great, work could be going well, your life could feel full—but if you don't have love in your life, your heart will be empty and you will feel incomplete.

Did you ever look at someone's life and wonder how they do it all? They have a successful career, active kids, a rigorous exercise routine, an updated wardrobe, a full social life, and important positions in the community. But something has to give. A person only has so much time and energy. The blanket of life is only so big. If it's pulled up over the head, the toes usually get exposed. Maybe they're not doing it all. Maybe the most important thing, their marriage, is not getting enough attention. Maybe all the external activity in their life is attempting to compensate for a lack of internal completion. Maybe they have everything except the most important thing—love.

Two wage-earner couples face an extra challenge. In the not-so-distant past, at least one spouse was available when the other finished work. But when both spouses in a marriage work, the marriage has to wait until both spouses are available. FedEx®, DSL, and all the other express business services allow us to accomplish more at a faster pace, but professional demands and personal ambitions result in most people working more and spending less time with their family. The problem is compounded by the fact that two wage earner families are forced to devote a lot of their non-working time to errands, food shopping, and childcare. By the end of the day, what time and energy is left for the marriage? For two wage earner marriages, to *put love first* is even more important and requires even more focus and discipline.

What do you do on the weekend? Do you spend more time with your extended family than with your spouse? Do you socialize for hours with your friends and then have nothing to say to your spouse? Who do you talk to at the party and what does that say about your priority? Is your extended family interfering with your marriage? Are you having intimate discussions with your sister that you should be having with your spouse? Talk with your spouse about how you can reorganize your days and weekends to reflect a higher value for each other and your marriage.

Some people get defensive about this topic because it threatens their lifestyle. Some marriages exist as a matter of convenience and compatibility rather than unity and deep love. Some people are satisfied because they are in a marriage that allows them to do what they want. Some people are more concerned about preserving their autonomy than committing to another person. But this is not love. This is selfish.

No matter how happy you might be with your

lifestyle—no matter how much you value your job, your golf game, your friends, or your exercise routine—everything would be so much more meaningful and fulfilling if you *put love first*.

If there were an emergency, you would drop everything to be with your spouse, right? I know it doesn't seem like an emergency. No one will die if you don't respond. But it is an emergency. It's a matter of love and life. Drop everything. Be with your spouse. *Put love first* and take the first step to transforming your marriage and your life.

How to be a Good Parent

Our children are precious to us. They warrant a great deal of our time and energy. But our spouse should come first.

Some parents make the mistake of devoting themselves so deeply to their children that they have no time or energy for their spouse. The irony is that unless your spouse comes first, you won't have a good marriage *or* be a good parent. For the sake of your marriage, and for the sake of your children, put your spouse first.

If you're driving your children all over town from one activity to the next and you're too exhausted to be with your spouse in the evening, consider cutting back on some of your children's after school activities. If you're spending so much money on your kids' clothes that you can't go on a weekend getaway with your spouse, it's time to start relying on hand-me-downs. If you're with your kids until 10:00 p.m. every night, it's time to enforce an earlier bedtime or teach them to be more independent.

Do you give all your time and energy to your children and have nothing left for your spouse? Does your parenting compromise your marriage? If this is the case, you need to change the way you parent so that your spouse has absolute and unchallenged top billing in your life. Don't worry about the consequences to your children—the best thing you can do for them is to have a great marriage.

It's probably safe to assume that you want your children to grow up and have true love, a lasting and fulfilling marriage, and ultimate fulfillment in life. Who is going to teach them how to achieve this in their life? You are! And, as is always the case, they won't learn it from what you say; they'll learn it from the life you lead. Your example is their teacher. The author, poet, and philosopher Ralph Waldo Emerson said, "Who you are speaks so loudly I can't hear a word you are saying." Whatever you want your children to achieve, you first have to achieve yourself. And the first step to achieving a phenomenal marriage is to prioritize your spouse higher than anything in the world—including your children.

Almost every evening my wife and I and our four children spend time together. The kids love this part of the day. But once a week, the babysitter arrives at 7:00 p.m. and my wife and I leave for the evening. The kids sometimes cry, but we leave anyway. They want to be with us *every* night, but they also want candy for dinner. It's our job to know what's best for them. And what's best for them is for us to spend one night each week alone.

Before my wife and I left for one of our private vacations (see *romantic retreats* below), our older son, who was six-years-old at the time, asked my wife why we were going away for three days without him. He was feeling sad. My wife responded, "Because Mommy and Daddy love each other and we want some time alone." He smiled and kissed us good-bye. He was going to miss us, but I think he understood. Were we being good parents? I believe that going away together for three days and that discussion my wife had with him prior to our departure had more impact on his development as a person (particularly as a future husband) than if we stayed home.

There is no doubt you should be willing to make changes for the sake of your children. And some of those changes will affect your marriage. But be careful that the changes you make do not change your priority.

There is nothing better than for children to be raised in

a home with parents who are soul mates. If children don't see true love, it won't matter how fashionably they dress or how well they play soccer. But if they witness you giving the highest priority to your spouse, you will give them the greatest gift of all—an example of how to succeed in love and marriage. And through love they will find completion in life, peace, and ultimate fulfillment.

Be a good parent—put your spouse first.

How to Actualize Love

Below are eight exercises to help you *put love first.* These are not *the* eight exercises to *put love first.* To *put love first* is more difficult than eight exercises. You could implement each exercise religiously and still fail to achieve the objective. In order to succeed with *put love first,* you need a *put love first* state-of-mind in addition to implementing the exercises below.

To cultivate a *put love first* state-of-mind, consider reviewing this chapter, listening to its audio versions, attending seminars based on the material, learning it with your spouse, meditating on the idea, and talking about it with your friends and family. To succeed with *put love first,* it's crucial to consistently remind yourself of the principle in as many ways as possible.

On the other hand, you cannot rely exclusively on the right attitude. Correct thinking is not enough to create phenomenal love. You need a discipline to help you actualize your intentions.

Marriage Fitness is like physical fitness. It's not enough to learn about it—you need an exercise routine too. It's a combination of the right consciousness and a discipline that produces results.

At this point in the chapter, you should be in a *put love first* state-of-mind. Here's an accompanying discipline of eight exercises.

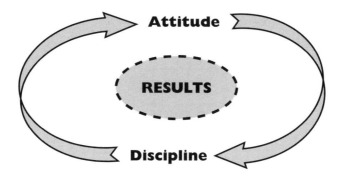

Talk Charge (Exercise 1.1)

Program: five times daily

When I use my cell phone a lot, I plug it into the car adapter when I drive to give it some "juice." When I drive short distances and use the cell phone a lot outside the car, I can't rely on these charges to keep the phone powered. However, it helps, and when I return home to charge the phone, it reaches full power more quickly.

You and your spouse will connect deeply when you spend quality time together, which I will address below. However, the modern life is a busy one, and most couples don't get the opportunity to spend enough quality time together. Therefore, I suggest at least five *talk charges* per day so that you stay connected and keep the power flowing between your cores.

A *talk charge* is any positive verbal interaction with your spouse that lasts a minimum of one minute. One minute is not a long time, but it must be positive, and you should have at least five *talk charges* per day.

There are so many *talk charge* possibilities. Have fun with them and be creative. Here are a few suggestions.

Tell your spouse about your dream when you wake up. Share something cute from the cereal box during breakfast. Phone mid-morning to share how your day is going. Phone again mid-afternoon just to say, "I love you." When you return home at the end of the day, don't open the mail or retrieve the phone messages—concentrate for at least one minute on your spouse first. If you have children, let them leave the table after dinner so you and your spouse can *talk charge* before cleaning up. Before you go to bed, look into the sky together and talk about the mystery of the universe. Or look at your children sleeping in their beds and talk about the miracle of life.

There is nothing special about the above examples; however, there are two things worth noting about them.

First, the topics were not practical. Talking about what's for dinner or who's going to pick up the kids will not be much of a charge for your marriage. Of course, you will need to have practical discussions throughout the day too, but don't count them as one of your *talk charges* unless you tack on one minute to your discussion and change the topic to something more personal. Remember, you're trying to make a soul connection.

Second, the examples I cited were spread out during the day. The objective is for you to stay connected and not be out of each other's lives for more than a few hours. Five phone calls at the end of the day after you realize you're behind on your *talk charges* is not in the spirit of the exercise.

When my wife and I began to *talk charge,* our marriage changed. Instead of being out of touch for hours, we continually connected. Instead of always talking about plans, the kids, money, dinner, shopping, and all the other logistical matters of life, we started to have fun and talk for the sake of being together.

I recommend at least five *talk charges* per day. That doesn't mean that each of you has to initiate five *talk charges,* but there should be five total between you. If you find that you are always the one reaching out, or always the one receiving, discuss that with your spouse and develop a strategy for better balance.

Does regular communication with your spouse feel like a burden? What if you're not a morning person and need your privacy until at least noon? What if you're too busy to stay in touch so frequently? What if you're the kind of person who gets immersed in their work and finds it disruptive to talk charge so frequently?

The *talk charge* exercise is designed to help you and your spouse adjust your priority. It's intended to help you be less self-centered and more love-centered (which ultimately is in your self interest). *Talk charges* give you and your spouse the opportunity everyday and throughout the entire day to *put love first*. And the higher you prioritize your spouse, the more you will connect with your spouse.

I love creative writing and I'm most productive when I immerse myself in the process for many hours consecutively. During the writing of this book, I wrote for twelve hours straight many days, stopping only to use the bathroom and to eat a banana. After a couple of hours I get into a zone where I become highly focused and extremely productive. That mental state is a special place for me. It feels great and it's where I do my best work. I try not to let anything interrupt it—except my wife. I always answer the phone when she calls. And sometimes I stop in the middle of a paragraph to touch base with her. We don't talk for long, but we connect. Is it disruptive? It is to my writing—but not to my marriage. And my marriage comes first.

Super Talk Charge (Exercise 1.2)

Program: once per week

Do you remember all the fascinating discussions you had with your spouse during your courtship? Hours upon hours you talked about... you probably can't even remember. Long into the night you conversed playfully, laughing, joking, and maybe even crying. These discussions created a bond between you—you fell in love.

It wasn't the topics you discussed that were important—it was the connection that talking created between you. There is an ancient tradition which teaches that words from the heart go into the heart. I would add—they join hearts.

A *super talk charge* is a twenty-five minute dialogue with

your spouse. Again, finances, in-laws, carpool, and all of life's logistical matters are off-limits. Talk about something personal, intimate, or romantic. Discuss your philosophy on life. Talk about your new hobby. Reminisce about your courtship. Share your feelings about anything. Get to know each other again. Have fun. Laugh together. Tell stories. Share jokes. Recite a poem.

I recommend at least one *super talk charge* per week. You can plan your *super talk charge* at the beginning of each week and schedule it in your calendar. Or you can be spontaneous. I try to keep my ears open for a *super talk charge* opportunity during the week. Sometimes my wife and I will be speaking about something and an interesting subject matter will come up. If I see we have the time, and I think it's an appropriate topic, I'll ask my wife what she thinks about the matter. I'll share my thoughts too. And before you know it, we're deep into a personal and intimate discussion.

A *super talk charge* will return you to the good-old-days when you and your spouse used to just talk. Do you remember how good it felt to just talk? Plan your *super talk charges*. Start talking again.

Touch Charge (Exercise 1.3)

Program: three times daily for each spouse

Retail clerks who graze the hands of customers when exchanging money are rated higher in customer service than those who do not. That's because physical contact affects how we feel about someone more than we realize. Touch creates more than just a physical connection.

Take note of how you feel next time someone gently puts their hand on your shoulder. Does it change the nature of the ensuing dialogue? Does it set the stage for a more pleasant discussion? How did their touch make you feel about them?

Many people complain that their spouse doesn't pay enough attention to them. It could be that they need to talk more. But they also probably need to touch more.

It's critical that you and your spouse touch each other regularly. Loving physical contact will create a connection between you. A gentle touch, a light stroke, or a warm kiss will connect your cores—it's a *touch charge.*

I suggest at least one *touch charge* in the morning and at least one more in the evening. You should try not to let more than twelve hours go by without being physically attentive to each other.

Unlike the *talk charge,* the three *touch charge* per day minimum applies to each spouse, which means that your marriage will experience six *touch charges* per day. If your spouse strokes your cheek while you're reading the newspaper and you respond by cuddling your spouse's hand, that counts as one *touch charge* for each of you.

Not all touches count. If you're taking the milk out of the refrigerator, and you accidentally bump into your spouse, it doesn't count as a *touch charge.* Also, degrading pats on the buttocks or pinches of the tummy don't count. A *touch charge* is not simply physical contact; it's positive, loving, physical contact.

My wife and I sometimes go out of our way, interrupting whatever we are doing, in order to caress each other. Sometimes the first thing I do in the morning when I wake up is roll over and kiss my wife. *Touch charges* keep us connected, physically and emotionally, and remind us that we are each other's priority.

Date Night (Exercise 1.4)

Program: once per week

I know a couple who were avid tennis players. They enjoyed tennis together throughout their courtship. Two years after they married, their marriage was in trouble. When was the last time they played tennis together? About two years ago. Is tennis only for dating?

How did you spend time together when you fell in love? How often did you go out when you were dating? It's time to start dating again—dating your spouse.

I don't think it's possible to succeed in marriage and experience true love without spending at least one night a week together.

Date night can work magic in your marriage if you follow four guidelines.

1. Get out of the house. No activity at home counts toward *date night*. Home will remind you of your practical and logistical matters. And if you have children… well, that's not a date.

2. No movies and no other entertainment that requires you to face in the same direction. You'll need to face each other. *You* are the entertainment. (There is an exception to this rule. If you have enough time, you can watch a movie and then spend a couple of hours talking over dinner. In any event, the point is that you need at least a couple of hours to really *be* together.)

3. Don't invite anyone else, and don't attend anything social. *Date night* is for you and your spouse *only*.

4. Schedule at least a couple of hours for *date night*. Don't tell your oldest child or the baby-sitter that you'll be back in an hour. *Date night* should be an evening.

Here's a suggestion for parents of small children. Like a physical fitness program, sometimes the hardest part of a Marriage Fitness program is mustering consistent inspiration. In other words, you may initiate *date night* this week, but what about next week and the week after? Can you do it consistently? Why test yourself? Here's an easy solution my wife and I discovered.

Rather than relying on your initiative each week, find a babysitter to commit to work the same hours every week. Our babysitter arrives at 7 p.m. every Wednesday night. We told her not to call to confirm—just come. Now we're set every week with date night. We don't have to find the inspiration to plan it—it's done! The burden is on us to cancel, not to plan.

Date night can help transform your marriage, but you have to tune into the spirit of the exercise. Two people can go on a date and not connect. If you go to the mall and read a magazine while your spouse tries on clothes—that's not a date. If you go to dinner and spend the evening talking to the waiter about how you want your meal prepared—it's not going to have much impact on your marriage. But if you help your spouse pick out an outfit and have fun offering your opinion, you will connect. If you talk over dinner about how you might prepare the dish at home, you will achieve the purpose of *date night*.

My wife and I had a swimming pool in our back yard when we lived in Florida. One *date night* we put candles around the pool and went for a night swim. We opened a bottle of wine and toasted each other while standing in the shallow end. We stared up into the starry sky and marveled at the planes that occasionally flew overhead. We talked about… what's the difference. It was an amazing evening, and it got better as the night went on.

Get creative with *date night*. Experiment and find fun things to do together. Take a board game to a coffee house. See if you can climb that tree on the corner of the block. Go to the local amusement park. Go race toy cars. Have a picnic in the park. Or just sit down for a quiet meal at a restaurant. Whatever you do, focus on each other. Date night is not about what you do; it's about *you*.

Romantic Retreat (Exercise 1.5)

Program: three times per year

In the corporate world, people use various means to stay connected: telephone, fax, email, meetings, lunches, conferences, water cooler chats, and memos. But the best corporations often plan a retreat. A corporate retreat is when people who work together go to a peaceful place for a few days and participate in activities designed to intensify their connection with each other.

How about a retreat for your marriage?

The *romantic retreat* is a private vacation getaway that will give you and your spouse the opportunity to escape all the distractions of home and work and immerse in each other for a few days. It's a time for long walks and long baths. It's a time to eat in the middle of the night and make love in the middle of the day. It's the ultimate exercise for your core connection.

As you might expect, no children, family, or friends can join you on your *romantic retreats*. Business conferences don't count unless you do your retreat before it begins or after it ends.

You might have some practical concerns about the *romantic retreat*. Let's explore the cost and the time away from work.

The *romantic retreat* should be at least three days and two nights. If you can afford the time and money, you can go for longer, but my experience is that you don't need more than three days and two nights to accomplish the objective and deeply connect.

If you schedule your retreats on the weekend, you probably only need to take one day off from work per retreat. Therefore, three romantic retreats per year require you to take three days off from work. If necessary, you could take unpaid vacation days.

If you're not able to take three days off from work, you need a new job. And I'm not kidding. If your work life doesn't allow you to tend to your marriage, then you need to find another way to make a living. If you can't earn as much money working somewhere else, consider getting a job making less money. If you can't live on less money, consider reducing your living expenses. I think you get the idea—*put love first*.

In terms of the cost, let me explain a little more about the *romantic retreat* and I think you'll see that it falls within even the most modest budgets.

The *romantic retreat* is not about the destination; it's about you. If you have money to spend, go ahead, knock yourself out and indulge. Try different spas or boutique hotels. Go to the Bahamas, Palm Springs, or Paris. Consult your travel agent for unusual romantic destinations and make reservations in the finest restaurants.

If your budget is limited, you can accomplish the objective just as well. All you need for a successful *romantic retreat* is your spouse and a hotel room, an inn, a log cabin, or a bed-and-breakfast.

It helps to be in a nice area where you can take walks, but you do not need to travel more than a few hours from your home and there is no need to spend money on airfare. In fact, if you're only going for three days and two nights, I recommend you find a destination as close as possible to your home so you maximize your time retreating and minimize your time traveling.

If you do a little research, you can usually find comfortable places that have special weekend packages. Hotels that cater to the business traveler are often very affordable on the weekends. Expand your search beyond hotels and check out the nearby inns and bed-and-breakfast establishments. These are actually better suited for a *romantic retreat.* Scan the travel section of your local newspaper periodically and plan your retreat when you see a good deal. Go online and visit some of the sites that specialize in travel. Do an internet search and see if you can find some bargains in your area. Subscribe to travel bargain email lists. Include your spouse in the search and have fun doing it together. You don't need a fancy place; you only need privacy, your spouse, and a will to connect.

When my wife and I do our *romantic retreats,* we bring our own food. We do this because we don't like to run-around to restaurants and it's also an effective cost cutting measure. If you don't want to prepare food or your room doesn't have a refrigerator, you can shop locally each day, have pizza delivered, or order from a take-out restaurant. If you plan to eat in the room, make sure it has at least a small table.

Since you have to eat when you're home too, the only additional cost for a low budget *romantic retreat* is your accommodations, which should be between fifty and one hundred dollars per night. Therefore, the cost for three low budget retreats per year (two nights each) is between $300 and $600—affordable for most budgets.

I want to warn you about the post *romantic retreat* blues. After three days of intimacy, peace and quiet, and relaxation, my wife and I return to dirty diapers, lots of phone messages, and full in-boxes. Life can change from serenity to stress very quickly. A *romantic retreat* is like a honeymoon three times a year. But like a honeymoon, it ends. Prepare yourselves. The key is to carry the energy of your retreat into the routine of your life and to maintain it using the exercises discussed in this section.

Begin planning your first *romantic retreat* now. It will be magical for your marriage.

Business Meeting (Exercise 1.6)

Program: once per week

Now that we've discussed the *romantic retreat,* let's get down to business.

You and your spouse probably have an endless list of logistical matters to discuss, including food shopping, budgeting, investments, vacation planning, car pooling, home maintenance, dry cleaning pick-up, bill paying, cooking, cleaning, party planning, holiday planning, and auto repair. It's not uncommon for matters like these to monopolize a couple's time and energy and for a marriage to become a partnership rather than a love affair.

Inevitably, you will need to discuss some of these matters with your spouse everyday. But how many of the logistical discussions you have with your spouse are urgent? In other words, how many of them could be postponed until a mutually agreeable time?

Unless it's urgent, I suggest you table as many "business" topics as possible for your weekly *business meeting.* This will ensure that as much of your week as possible will be love and not business. You can keep a running agenda all week long as you think of topics you need to discuss, and then discuss them all at once with your spouse during your *business meeting.*

When business matters are spontaneously scattered in discussions you have with your spouse throughout the entire week, it gives your marriage a business flavor. But if you can table as many of these discussions as possible and fill those moments with love instead—wow. I can't describe what a difference this has made in our marriage.

When my wife and I discuss our agenda during our *business meeting,* I'm not distracted by work, she doesn't have kids hanging on her, we've agreed to not answer the phone, and neither of us have anywhere else to go because we blocked out the time for each other. It's really an amazing discipline that has changed our life.

In addition to going through an agenda, my wife and I confirm the dates and times of all our commitments including *date night, pick a hobby—any hobby* (see Chapter 6), and our next *business meeting.* This avoids confusion about our weekly plans.

Since it is a business meeting, no one's feelings get hurt because of the agenda. Sometimes when couples begin an interaction, they are approaching the encounter with different expectations. You want to be intimate, but your spouse wants to discuss the weekly budget. This is a recipe for conflict. But when you schedule a weekly *business meeting,* no one can be disappointed because they were expecting a romantic encounter. A *business meeting* is a clearly delineated island of time designated for business purposes.

Before you begin your *business meeting,* make sure your children are asleep, agree to not answer the telephone, and turn off the TV. Sit at a table with pen and pad and go through your agenda. Make notes, divide responsibility, and agree to update each other either at the next *business meeting* or before then if necessary.

The *business meeting* is truly a powerful exercise. You probably only need to schedule about forty-five minutes. It's not a long time, but it changes the tone of the entire week and provides you with more opportunities to connect in love rather than discuss business.

Photo Opp (Exercise 1.7)

Program: office and wallet, minimum

This simple exercise will remind you of your spouse and help you connect even when you're out of touch.

The idea of the *photo opp* is to put photos of your spouse in locations that you frequent but which your spouse does not. The most obvious examples are your office, your wallet, and your gym locker. If you don't already have photos of your spouse in these places, consider putting them there now. Are there other locations that make sense for you to hang photos of your spouse? If so, put them there too.

I was once in a person's office who proudly hung autographed photos of famous people. There were more photos of the President than there were of his wife. There's nothing wrong with autographed photos of famous people, but I remember being with this man and wondering which relationship was more important to him.

Having photos of your spouse in strategic places reminds you and is a statement to everyone else that your spouse is the most important person in your life.

Ever since I was a child, my stepfather had a photo collection of my mother on his office walls. There are no family photos there—only photos of my mother. There must be close to thirty 8-by-10 framed photos. It's like a shrine. I didn't appreciate it when I was a child, but I realize now that those photos are a powerful testimony to the space that my mother holds in her husband's heart. More than thirty years later, all the same photos still hang on that wall.

Unlike the *business meeting,* this exercise is easy to implement. Don't miss your *photo opp.*

Birthday Party (Exercise 1.8)

Program: once per year per spouse

You may think that having a birthday party for your spouse is not a unique suggestion. You may wonder how it could help your marriage or create a connection between you and your spouse. You may even know couples who threw lavish birthday parties for each other but are now split up. But there is a unique element to the *birthday party* that is original and that makes it effective. That unique element is the invite list.

Plan an amazing *birthday party* for your spouse. Pick a fine restaurant, hire a caterer, or cook a gourmet meal. Decorate your house or the restaurant table with streamers and balloons. Make special signs. Buy a thoughtful gift. Find the perfect card. Hire entertainment. Go all out in every way within whatever budget you can afford. And then invite your spouse—only your spouse!

"All that work and I'm only inviting one person?" you might ask. That's right. You're inviting only one person—the most important person in the world.

If the President of the United States offered to spend his birthday at your house, how many people would you invite?

The more important the people, the smaller you want the party. So for the most important person, make it a private affair.

You won't have anyone else to greet, cook for, serve, talk to, or hug—your spouse will have all of you and you will have all of your spouse. That's putting love first.

It's reasonable to plan an extravagant party when the invite list includes lots of family and friends. It would be unreasonable to do so and then invite only one person. Be unreasonable. It's very romantic.

I'm not opposed to celebrations that include family and friends. They can be a good idea too. But schedule your private celebration first. Make it clear that it is your priority.

I recommend scheduling the *birthday party* on *date night*. Or, better yet, schedule it during one of your *romantic retreats*. This prevents your schedule from getting stressed at birthday time.

The Time for Love

How much time does it take to implement these Marriage Fitness exercises? Let's calculate based on the above program.

Exercise	Program	Hours per Year
1.1 Talk Charge	5 minutes/day	30
1.2 Super Talk Charge	25 minutes/week	22
1.3 Touch Charge	3 times daily/spouse	1
1.4 Date Night	2 hours/week	104
1.5 Romantic Retreat	100 hours/year	100
1.6 Business Meeting	45 minutes/week	39
1.7 Photo Opp	once per spouse	1
1.8 Birthday Party	once per year per spouse	5
TOTAL:		**302 Hours/Year**

It takes about 302 hours each year to implement the above program.

There are 8760 hours in a year (assuming 365 days), which means that it would take a little more than three percent of your time to *put love first*—to take the first step toward connecting at your core, transforming your marriage, and discovering ultimate fulfillment in life.

What do you think? Is it worth it?

The average person spends between ten and twenty percent of their time watching TV. I'll leave the commentary to you.

If you had to do all the above exercises for your job, for your community, or for your kids, would you do it? Could you do it? I bet you would. I bet you would make it happen.

For some reason, we tend not to put the same energy into our marriage. But we should. Take this discipline seriously. Make it happen. Make it your priority.

First Things First

Let's do an imaginary exercise. Imagine a bucket filled to its top with large rocks. If I asked you if it were full, you would probably respond "yes." But I could fill the bucket further by pouring in smaller rocks and letting them settle between the larger ones. If I did that and asked you again if the bucket were full, this time you would probably respond "no," and explain that sand could be poured into the bucket to fill the remaining gaps. If I did that and once again asked you if the bucket were full, you might suggest that water could be added to further fill the bucket. Finally, after filling the bucket with big rocks, small rocks, sand, and water, the bucket would be full—nothing else could be added.

What's the point? Since we are talking about priorities, you might think that the point is that if you try hard enough you can always find a little more time to squeeze in what's most important. That answer makes sense, but it's not the most profound point.

The point is that if we didn't put the big rocks in first, they would not have fit at all. What are the big rocks in your life? What's really important? What really matters in the end? What will bring you ultimate meaning and fulfillment? The answer is love. Put it first.

Summary

Step one of the MarriageMax™ 4-step Plan for connecting your cores and building phenomenal love is to make your spouse and your marriage the absolute highest priority in your life bar none. In other words—step one is to *put love first.*

96

To succeed with *put love first* requires the right attitude and an exercise discipline. Here are eight exercises to help you *put love first.*

1. Talk charge
2. Super talk charge
3. Touch charge
4. Date night
5. Romantic retreat
6. Business meeting
7. Photo opp
8. Birthday party

FREE Online Supplement

**"How to get over your past
and past your hurt"**
Available now at www.Marriagemax.com/past.asp

The MarriageMax™ 4-Step Plan

1. Put Love First
2. **Give Presence**
3. Move from Me to We
4. Save Yourself

Chapter 5

GIVE PRESENCE

Love and giving go hand-in-hand.

My wife and I gave each other many gifts during our courtship. I gave her flowers and Robin Williams's videos (her favorite actor). She gave me sport shirts and home cooked meals. We fell in love, and giving was one way we expressed our sentiments.

Of course, my wife and I are not unusual. It's common for people in love to give to each other. Almost every retail shop offers gift wrapping because many customers buy for someone other than themselves. FTD, Hallmark, and diamond jewelers built businesses helping people express their love through giving. When you give, you make a statement. Giving says "I love you."

Unfortunately, after the first few years of a marriage, giving between spouses tends to decline. How many husbands after a few years of marriage give their wives flowers for no particular reason? As the passion of love fades, so does the desire to express it through giving. Usually, the more love between spouses, the more they give to each other. And the less love between spouses, the less they give to each other.

Let's explore the relationship between love and giving further. What *really* is the correlation between them? Is there something about the dynamic between love and giving that can help you and your spouse connect at your cores and create phenomenal love?

Connecting through Giving

When I lived in New York, I had a friend who bought a used sports car. The car was nothing special; however, over time, he began to fix it up. He shampooed the inside, painted and waxed the outside, added distinctive hub caps, ordered personalized licensed plates, painted pinstripes, installed body side moldings, and put in a new stereo system. Every Sunday he worked on his car, and each week he was more excited than the last. He started to refer to his car as "she," and occasionally he gave it a love tap on the hood. No one else was allowed to drive the car, and everyone had to brush off their shoes before getting in. And then one day he said it—"I love this car."

My friend didn't love his car when he bought it. What changed? And how does a person fall in love with a car—an inanimate object?

My friend loved his car because he continually gave to his car. Giving builds a connection between the giver and the receiver. Giving creates love. And the relationship between giving and the experience of love is so powerful that it works even with inanimate objects.

What do you feel a strong affinity to in your life? Do you give a lot of yourself to it?

It's normal to give to whoever you love. But the dynamic between love and giving works the other way too. You will love whoever you give to.

In the first couple of years of marriage, it's natural to give as a result of the love you feel. But after the first couple of years, you need to give not *because* you love, but *in order* to "make" love. Rather than love inspiring you to give, giving inspires you to love. And the more you give, the more you will love. As the author Leo Tolstoy said, "We do not love people so much for the good they have done us, as for the good we have done them."

Step two of the MarriageMax™ 4-Step Plan for connecting your cores and building phenomenal love is to give to your spouse—specifically to *give presence*.

100

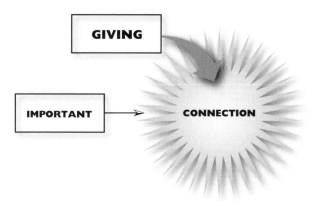

Becoming a Part of Your Spouse

How does the dynamic between love and giving work? Why does giving create love?

To understand, let's explore why my friend loved his car. Why did giving to his car result in him connecting to it so deeply?

The fact that my friend would not let anyone drive his car is insightful. Why was it a problem to let someone take it for a spin? The worst case scenario was an accident and the insurance company pays to repair the damage. In no time, the car would be like new again. What was the big deal?

The problem was that an accident would not have only damaged the car, but also his connection to it. The car could have been replaced or repaired, but his connection to *his* work would have taken hours to fix. It's not the car that my friend protected so carefully; it was his connection to it. And that can't be replaced by an insurance company. That only comes from giving.

Just as my friend connected with his car, you and your spouse can connect with each other. In fact, if a person can connect with a car through unilateral giving, imagine the depth of connection you and your spouse can create by giving reciprocally.

Giving creates a deep connection. The best example is the love and deep connection that parents feel for their children. Parenting is an exercise in perpetual unconditional giving. And there is almost no greater love than the love a parent feels for their child. Interestingly, for those of us who are both parents and children, although we may love our parents, it does not compare to the love we feel for our children. The love a parent has for their child is much greater than the love a child feels for their parent because parents give more to their children than children give to their parents.

Giving Great Sex

In the most primitive way, Mother Nature teaches that giving between a man and a woman creates an intense connection between them.

There is no feeling comparable to the safety, completeness, and ecstasy at the climax of sex. It is there that we feel most connected physically, spiritually, and emotionally.

At the peak of love making, when the depth of connection between a man and a woman is most intense, a man and a woman give to each other. Man gives woman his body part, his semen, and the potential for new life. It's easy for a man to give to a woman during love making. But neither the man nor the woman will experience the potential of love making and the possibility of ultimate connectedness unless the woman has the opportunity to give too. If a man is selfish and only interested in his pleasure, love making will not only be unfulfilling for the woman, but to some extent for the man too. The greatest sexual pleasure for a man is not when he gives of himself; it's when he gives of himself and his wife simultaneously gives to him.

When a woman completely opens herself up, physically and emotionally and gives all of herself during love making, and when her husband reciprocates, at that point life is complete for both man and woman and their depth of connection can be expressed only with a primal scream. In the most natural way that a man and a woman relate, Mother Nature is teaching that giving creates true love and a profound connection.

Giving Your Needs Met

There is a wonderful story about one of King Arthur's knights of the Round Table whose name was Sir Gawain. Sir Gawain was a handsome man who could have married any beautiful women in the kingdom. Out of loyalty to King Arthur, Sir Gawain, in exchange for information that would save the king's life, agreed to marry Ragnell, who was hideous.

On their wedding night, Ragnell said, "You have kept your promise and much more. You have never shown me pity or revulsion. All I will ask of you is one kiss." Without hesitation, Sir Gawain leaned over, closed his eyes, and kissed Ragnell. When he opened his eyes, lying beside him was a beautiful woman. Sir Gawain said, "Who are you? And where is my wife? Is this some kind of sorcery?" The woman said, "Gawain, I am your wife, Ragnell. It is time to tell you my story."

Ragnell told him about her evil stepbrother, Sir Gromer, who hated her because of her beauty and because she was not obedient to him. Sir Gromer complained about Ragnell to his mother, an evil sorceress, who turned Ragnell into the most hideous woman in the kingdom.

Ragnell continued, "There is a second part of the curse I must share with you. Since you have treated me with love and not resentment or pity, I am allowed to give you a choice. I can be a beautiful woman by day, so that all may admire me and consider you a lucky man, but I would become once more the ugly Ragnell by night, when we lie with each other. Or I could be the ugly Ragnell by day, only to once again become the beautiful woman you see before you at night. Which would you prefer?"

Sir Gawain answered immediately, "This should not be my choice but yours. You must choose for yourself. I will accept either decision, as long as it is your will."

With his response, the curse was lifted and Ragnell was beautiful day and night.

Sir Gawain was asked to decide which of his needs he wanted met—public honor or personal pleasure. Sir Gawain chose neither. He chose to meet the needs of his wife. And when he chose to meet the needs of his wife, *both* his needs were met. Sir Gawain got personal pleasure *and* public honor.

If Sir Gawain selected one of his needs, the other would have remained unfulfilled. Ironically, his concern for the needs of his wife resulted in *his* complete fulfillment.

The story of Sir Gawain and Ragnell is reflective of a fascinating and insightful dynamic in your marriage too. If you try to get your needs met, you will never be completely fulfilled. But if you meet the needs of your spouse, all your needs will be met. How could that be? Why does it work that way?

The answer returns us to the core ideology of Marriage Fitness. Remember the discussion in Chapter 1 about what you *really* want and need for fulfillment in life? It's love. And love is a result of a deep core connection between you and your spouse. If you can create that connection, you will have everything in life—all your needs will be met. But interestingly, the way to get all your needs met is to meet the needs of your spouse because giving, not receiving, is what builds love. In other words, the way to consummate a connection with your spouse, the result of which will be your fulfillment, is not to focus on your fulfillment but to focus on giving to your mate and ensuring their fulfillment. Ironically, if you try to get your needs met, you will fail. If you give to your spouse, you will create a deep connection, which is love, and you will get everything you need.

Most people make the mistake of jockeying with their spouse to try to get their needs met. But while each spouse is manipulating the other to get what they need, no one is satisfied. People confuse what they think they need with their ultimate need. Only love satisfies. Everything else is counterfeit.

There was a time when my wife and I had a long list of things we wanted from each other. We fought a lot and we did everything we could to get the other to give us what we wanted. But the harder we tried, the less we got. The only thing we got more of was stress and disappointment.

Ironically, my wife and I finally got our needs met when we stopped focusing on getting our needs met and started focusing on creating a core connection. And one of the practices that created that core connection was giving to each other. The more we gave to each other, the more we connected, and the more we got what we really needed. Giving got our needs met.

I can't remember most of the things I fought so hard to get. I'm not sure if my list of needs were met or not. It doesn't matter. My ultimate need was met, and that changed everything. Love conquers all.

Too many people spend their lives trying to get their needs met. It never works. You can't *get* your needs met. You can only *give* your needs met.

Beyond the Mountain of Darkness

There is an ancient tradition which teaches that Alexander of Macedonia, who was a world-conqueror, once traveled beyond the Mountains of Darkness to a kingdom called Cassia. The King of Cassia offered to show Alexander of Macedonia his system of justice.

At that time two men came before the court. One man bought a plot of land from his neighbor and discovered a hidden treasure buried in it. The buyer claimed that he didn't intend to buy the treasure and didn't even know that it was on the land. Therefore, he insisted that the treasure belonged to his neighbor, the seller. The seller, on the other hand, claimed that his intention was to sell the land and all that it contained, and therefore the treasure belonged to the buyer.

The dispute was resolved when the King of Cassia discovered that the buyer and the seller had a son and daughter

105

of marriageable age. The king decided that they would marry, that the families would be joined, and that the buyer and the seller would be *both* givers and receivers of the treasure.

If either neighbor in the story tried to get the treasure, only one of them would have been satisfied, and their relationship would have been soured. Since they tried to give it to each other, they both received it, and, most importantly, they created love in the process.

On the Cassia side of the Mountains of Darkness, where people are inclined to give rather than take, there is love and satisfaction. There is satisfaction both because people experience the love and depth of connection that is their ultimate yearning and because, ironically, in a community of givers, everyone gets their needs met.

Move the energy in your home to the Cassia side of the Mountains of Darkness. Make it a place of giving, and you and your spouse will be joined in love and get everything you ever wanted.

In-to-me-see

My wife once asked me to scratch an itch on her back. I started in the middle of her back and then she guided me. "A little to the right," she said. "Higher, higher," she said. "Now a little to the left," she continued. But I wasn't scratching in the right spot. "Just scratch where it itches already," she finally said in frustration.

In order to give to your spouse, you have to know what your spouse needs. Where is your spouse's itch?

I once heard a story about a couple who were in therapy after twenty years of marriage. The wife complained to the therapist that her husband never said he loved her anymore. The therapist turned to the husband and said, "So? Is it true? Do you love her?" The husband turned to his wife and said, "I told you twenty years ago that I loved you. If I changed my mind, I would have let you know."

I didn't share this story to show the difference between men and women. My point is *not* that the man in the story was not expressive (although that's true). My point is that the woman in the story never expressed her needs in twenty years of marriage. She never told her husband that she wanted him to say, "I love you." Never mind that such a thing should be obvious. For whatever reason, to her husband it was not. And she never made it clear.

In order for you and your spouse to give to each other regularly, you have to tell each other about your needs. You have to get to know each other very well.

The problem in many marriages is that people don't know each other. They live together, but they're not intimate. Intimacy means having knowledge. The phonetic of the word "intimacy" gives insight into its meaning—in-to-me-see. Can you see deep into your spouse? Can your spouse see deep into you? Do you have intimate knowledge of each other? Do you know what to give to each other? Do you understand each other's needs?

To create love, you need knowledge of each other. The word the Bible uses for sexual intimacy is the same word it uses for knowledge. Both offer the opportunity to give. Both are a doorway to love.

Do you remember your courtship? Do you remember learning something about your spouse and responding with a thoughtful gift or gesture? When I learned that my wife wanted a pure white fluffy spa-like towel (something you don't find in a home with four little kids), I brought one home. The gesture took five minutes and cost six dollars. It meant the world. She got the towel she wanted. We both got the love we need.

Did you stop thinking about how you could give and start thinking about how you could get? If you want your needs met, get to know your spouse's needs and start giving.

Give Presence Marriage Assessment I

This assessment measures how well you know your spouse and your ability to give them what they want.

Answer the questions below and then ask your spouse how many questions you answered correctly. Calculate your score and compare it with the assessment scale below.

		Correct	Incorrect
1.	What's your spouse's favorite color?	☐	☐
2.	What's your spouse's favorite city to visit? _____	☐	☐
3.	What's your spouse's favorite vacation destination? _____	☐	☐
4.	What's your spouse's favorite restaurant? _____	☐	☐
5.	What's your spouse's favorite type of food?_____	☐	☐
6.	What's your spouse's favorite home cooked meal?_____	☐	☐
7.	What's your spouse's favorite dessert?	☐	☐
8.	What's your spouse's favorite holiday?	☐	☐
9.	What's your spouse's most dreaded holiday?_____	☐	☐
10.	Who's your spouse's best friend?	☐	☐
11.	Who's your spouse's favorite relative?	☐	☐
12.	What's your spouse's favorite clothing store? _____	☐	☐

	Correct	Incorrect
13. What size shirt/blouse does your spouse wear? _____	☐	☐
14. What size pants/skirt does your spouse wear? _____	☐	☐
15. What size suit/dress does your spouse wear? _____	☐	☐
16. What size shoe does your spouse wear? _____	☐	☐
17. What's your spouse's favorite thing for YOU to wear? _____	☐	☐
18. What's your spouse's favorite day of the week? _____	☐	☐
19. What's the most relaxing thing for your spouse? _____	☐	☐
20. What's most stressful for your spouse? _____	☐	☐
21. What's your spouse's most dreaded chore? _____	☐	☐
22. What's your spouse's pet peeve? _____	☐	☐
23. What's the one thing your spouse has always wanted? _____	☐	☐
24. Who's your spouse's favorite actor? _____	☐	☐
25. What's your spouse's favorite movie? _____	☐	☐
26. Who's your spouse's favorite artist? _____	☐	☐
27. Who's your spouse's favorite musician? _____	☐	☐
28. What type of music does your spouse like the best? _____	☐	☐
29. What is your spouse's favorite way of making love? _____	☐	☐

	Correct	Incorrect
30. How often per month or week does your spouse like to make love? _____	☐	☐
31. Who is your spouse's favorite author? _____	☐	☐
32. What's your spouse's all-time favorite book? _____	☐	☐
33. What type of books does your spouse like to read? _____	☐	☐
34. What is your spouse's favorite spectator sport? _____	☐	☐
35. Who is your spouse's favorite sports hero? _____	☐	☐
36. What's your spouse's favorite sports team? _____	☐	☐
37. What is your spouse's favorite hobby? _____	☐	☐
38. At what temperature does your spouse like the thermostat set? _____	☐	☐
39. What is your spouse's favorite topic of discussion? _____	☐	☐
40. If your spouse had an extra $100 per week to spend, what would your spouse choose to spend it on? _____	☐	☐
41. If your spouse was given one million dollars and had to spend it within one week, what would be the first high ticket item your spouse would buy?_____	☐	☐
42. Which type of vacation does your spouse prefer? a) Sun, fun, and relax b) Sightseeing c) Outdoor adventure	☐	☐

	Correct	Incorrect

43. The best type of gift for my spouse is something:
    a) Practical
    b) Sentimental
    c) Just what they asked for
    d) A surprise

44. My spouse prefers to wear/buy:
    a) Gold
    b) Silver
    c) Platinum

Number of Correct Answers

0–19: OUT OF SHAPE. You have a lot to learn about your spouse. Ask more questions. Pay closer attention during conversation. Concentrate during your *intimacy interview* (see below).

20–31: AVERAGE. You know enough to give some of the right things, but you could do better. Review the questions you got wrong and try to identify areas about your spouse where your knowledge is lacking. Make an effort to learn about them. Focus on them during your *intimacy interview* (see below).

32–44: MARRIAGE FITNESS CHAMPION. Your knowledge of your spouse will make *giving* much easier. Keep building your knowledge bank. *Giving* based on fresh understandings is very powerful, so don't rest on your laurels.

Intimacy Interview (Exercise 2.1)

Program: one per spouse per year

Did you ever hear the question, "Does a tree that falls make noise if no one is around to hear it?" So many things in life require pairs in order for them to be actualized. For example, a teacher needs a student. A person may have the potential to teach, but a person only becomes a teacher when he teaches a student.

In the same way, a giver needs a receiver. You may want to give your spouse something, but if your spouse doesn't want to receive it, you can't give it.

Imagine my wife and I want to surprise you with a 5 course, home cooked gourmet meal. I call you on the phone and ask you to come to my house at 7 p.m. because we have something important to talk to you about. You don't know what the agenda is nor do you know how long the discussion will last. Since you didn't have dinner, you stop at a fast food restaurant and eat a couple of burgers and French fries in the car while you drive to our house. Upon your arrival, my wife and I escort you to our dining room and surprise you with a beautifully set table and a 5 course, home cooked gourmet meal. We're so excited to give you dinner, but we cannot. We went to great lengths to give you something special, but we forgot to do the most important thing. We forgot to make sure you would want it.

In order for you and your spouse to give to each other, you need to know each other's needs. Don't wait twenty years for one of you to tell the therapist that the other never says, "I love you." Tell each other what you want.

How do you and your spouse get a list of things that the other wants? How do you know what to give? You have to ask. I suggest *intimacy interviews.*

An *intimacy interview* is when one spouse interviews the other about their wants. After you interview each other, you and your spouse will have a comprehensive list of each other's wants—a list of things to give to each other.

Here are some logistical suggestions for a successful interview. If the interview is done properly, it could take a couple of hours. Therefore, I suggest only one interview per evening. Try to schedule the second interview within ten days of the first. Whoever conducts the interview should have a laptop computer or a pen and pad so that there will be a list you can refer to and edit over the years. Make sure the kids are asleep and the TV is off. Agree with your spouse that you will not answer the phone during the interview or accept any interruptions other than emergencies. Put some refreshments on the table, light a candle, and dim the lights.

Begin each interview by discussing its purpose. You can read passages from this chapter to remind each other of the main points.

The interviewer should encourage the interviewee to be as open and detailed as possible. Remind each other that this is your chance to ask for everything you ever wanted.

The interviewer should only ask questions and seek to clarify their spouse's desires. The interviewer should not make statements, comments, or remarks of any kind. In terms of facial expressions and body language, the interviewer should react only in a neutral or positive way, and be careful not to discourage the interviewee from exposing themselves.

The interviewee, on the other hand, should not ask questions. The interviewee should remain focused on exploring their desires.

Sex is often a difficult topic to discuss openly. Help each other with this topic. Extend a special effort to be sensitive to each other and work hard to create a safe environment. The interviewer can help by asking specific questions. It's much easier to respond to an inquiry than it is to volunteer information.

When you get to the topic of sex, you might try turning off the lights and lighting a candle. It feels much safer to share in the dark.

The interviewer can begin the interview by simply asking what the other wants. The interviewee should download everything they want in life. The questions and answers should be as detailed as possible. For example, if one of you says you want a back rub after love-making, you should discuss how hard or soft, with or without moisturizer, and what part of the back is the most favorite. If one of you wants the house to be a certain temperature, discuss exactly how to set the thermostat.

Love is in the details. Ask about details. Get intimate. You and your spouse should know each other better than anyone else in the world. You should share with each other things you wouldn't dream of sharing with anyone else. Let it all out. Let your spouse in. Knowledge is love. Give each other knowledge. Give each other love. Give each other the opportunity to give.

The main purpose of asking for what you want is not so you get what you want; it's so your spouse can give you what you want. Giving creates love. That's what's important. Getting is just a bonus. When you interview your spouse, don't worry about not being able to meet some or even many of your spouse's desires. The purpose of the interview is not that your spouse gets what your spouse wants; it's that you have as many opportunities as possible to give what your spouse wants. The fact that your spouse will get some needs met will not affect your marriage much. You giving your spouse what your spouse wants, on the other hand, will transform it.

If you earn a school teacher's salary and your spouse is asking for a diamond ring, don't worry about it. It's not a problem that your spouse will not get a diamond ring. The problem is that you can't give it. But that only means that you need to look for other opportunities to give. The idea of the *intimacy interview* is to get to know your spouse so well that you have an endless list of opportunities to give.

Use the following categories to help you during your interviews. Probe each other about each category.

1. Vacation and Travel
2. Conversation
3. Children & Parenting
4. Family Time
5. Holidays & Special Occasions
6. Entertainment
7. Clothes & Jewelry
8. Food & Cooking
9. Dining Out
10. Exercise
11. Personal Growth
12. Education
13. Food Shopping
14. House Repairs & Maintenance
15. House Organization
16. Money & Investing
17. Sex
18. Religion & Spirituality
19. House Furniture
20. House Temperature
21. Extended Family
22. Books
23. Music
24. Sports
25. Physical Signs of Affection
26. Household Chores
27. Timeliness
28. Personal Hygiene
29. Car Temperature
30. Business/Profession

Within each of the categories, use these sub categories to probe deeper:

1. Frequency
2. Destination
3. Style
4. Class
5. Length
6. Types
7. Topics

When you're finished interviewing your spouse, summarize your notes and review them carefully. Mark your spouse's desires that you can accommodate immediately. Don't worry about what you can't give—focus on what you can give. Next, make a special note next to the desires that offer you a daily opportunity to give. For example, if your spouse wants you to make coffee in the morning, make that a priority to accommodate.

If you're not used to being attentive to your spouse's needs, giving regularly may be a big lifestyle change. Feel free to implement changes slowly. As you begin to give more, you will experience the impact that giving has on your marriage and you'll be motivated to find more ways to give. Therefore, I suggest you review your notes from the interview each week for at least two months. Continue to look for new ways to give to your spouse.

You and your spouse will want to make sure your lists remain private. Needless to say, any breach of confidentiality or carelessness with the list could destroy the very bond the lists are intended to help you create.

Conduct an *intimacy interview* once each year. Depending on how much you and your spouse's needs change in the years following your first interview, subsequent interviews could be brief reviews or another lengthy process. In either case, the two most important things to probe and listen for after the initial interview are new needs and needs that your spouse shared in previous years that you weren't able to fulfill. New needs are a great opportunity to give in a fresh way. All giving cultivates a core connection; however, there is something special about giving in new ways.

Give (Exercise 2.2)

Program: minimum three per day

After you have an inventory of giving opportunities, start exercising *gives*. Just as you need to eat regularly to give your body nourishment, you need to *give* to your spouse regularly to give your marriage its fuel.

You should *give* to your spouse at least three times per day. Spread your giving throughout the day so that your core connection is constantly being renewed. Try to *give* at least once in the morning before you part for the day. (The combination of a *give, talk charge,* and *touch charge* is an amazing way to start every day. Beginnings are important. A good start sets the tone for your entire day together.)

Try to vary the way you *give*. The benefit of giving in the same way each day is that once you get into the habit (of making the coffee for example), there will be an automatic daily charge to your core connection. However, the problem is that giving in the same way everyday can lose its freshness.

It's too easy to begin to make the coffee not as an act of giving, but simply out of habit. Inconsistency in your intention is definitely not a reason to stop giving; however, it is a reason to give in more unusual ways that will be new and exciting for you and your spouse.

Review your list regularly in search of new ways to *give* to your spouse. For example, maybe your spouse asked to be read a love poem occasionally. This is probably not something you will do everyday, but it would add a special spark to any day.

Be careful to *give* only what your spouse wants. Giving your spouse something you want them to have doesn't count unless it is also on their list. Giving your spouse a membership to Weight Watchers if they don't want to diet will not be helpful.

The Most Important Thing to Give

You could conduct your *intimacy interviews* and *give* to each other three times each day and still not maximize the value of your giving. You could give everything to your spouse and still not give the most important thing.

In order to make music, you need to play the right notes. But to make *beautiful* music, you need rhythm too. To connect with your spouse, you need to *give,* but to deeply connect you need something else too. What's the rhythm of giving? When you give, what is the most important thing to give? It's you. Let me explain.

Imagine you receive a gift-wrapped package in the mail. What's the first thing you do? Do you immediately rip it open to see what's inside? No. The first thing you do is look for a return address, right? If there was no return address, you would look for a gift card. You'd probably be thinking, "Who sent this to me?"

Why does it matter who sent you the gift? What if I promised you that whoever sent you this gift would receive your appreciation? Would you be willing to forget about who sent you the gift and just enjoy it? You would not.

117

Give Presence Marriage Assessment II

Rate your giving to your spouse in each category below on a scale from 1-10. Calculate your score and compare it with the assessment scale below.

_____ SPECIAL OCCASION GIFTS. Do you buy your spouse a gift for their birthday, your anniversary, and other special holidays and occasions? How thoughtful is the gift? Did you just buy anything, or could your spouse feel your presence in it?

_____ SURPRISE GIFTS. Do you give your spouse surprise gifts? Will you sometimes go out of your way for no logical reason to bring your spouse a gift?

_____ CHORES. Do you give your spouse a break by sometimes doing their chores? How often? Do you have to be asked or do you sometimes surprise your spouse? Do you expect the same in return or do you unselfishly give? Are you tuned-in to when your spouse really needs a break? Do you know when your spouse needs your help? What about all the chores that are not clearly your responsibility or your spouses? Do you just do them when it needs to be done so your spouse doesn't have to? Do you change the diaper or the light bulb without being asked?

_____ FREE TIME. Do you give your spouse free time for themselves by relieving them of obligations or chores? Do you ever take the kids for an afternoon so your spouse can do their shopping, catch up on their work, or just relax? Are you tuned-in to when your spouse needs some free time to themselves?

_____ YOUR TIME. Do you give your time to your spouse? Do you listen when your spouse tells you something? Do you ask questions and take the time to show interest?

_____ SEX. Are you a giver? Are you concerned about meeting your spouse's needs? Do you ask how you can meet their needs? Do you ask if you have met their needs? Does satisfying sex to you mean pleasing your partner too, or do you measure it according to your pleasure?

_____ YOUR PRESENCE. How much of your heart and soul is in your giving? Can your partner feel your presence in your presents?

| | **YOUR TOTAL SCORE** |

0–25. OUT OF SHAPE. Try to internalize the discussion in this chapter, do the intimacy interview, and start giving. I bet this assessment touched on some sore spots in your marriage. Make note of them and try to address them.

26–55. AVERAGE. You understand that giving is important, but something is holding you back from complete unconditional giving. What is it? Do you need more knowledge of your spouse? Are there particular areas where you are not giving? Can you change that?

56–70. MARRIAGE FITNESS CHAMPION. Good work. You must know your spouse well and give often. Did you rate yourself accurately? Ask your spouse if they would agree with your ratings. How can you give even more?

Why? Because a gift's meaning comes from its giver. What really makes a gift special is not what it is, but who gave it to you.

Imagine that Glenn and Patty have been dating for a while. Glenn feels strongly about Patty, but Patty continues to go out with Glenn not because of her feelings for him but because she enjoys the expensive restaurants he's able to afford.

One night while they're sitting in the corner of a dimly lit five-star restaurant with candles burning on the table, Glenn reaches into his coat pocket and places before Patty a small black-felt jewelry box. Patty gets very nervous and sits back on her chair. Glenn opens the box and reveals the sparkle of a spectacular sapphire ring. The ring is beautiful, but Patty can't accept it. She's not interested in the ring because she's not interested in Glenn.

Can you imagine wearing an expensive piece of jewelry given to you by someone you don't love? You probably wouldn't do it. Why not? A beautiful ring looks beautiful regardless of who gave it to you. What if someone you loved gave you the same ring? Now you would wear it with joy, right? Why? What's the difference?

Imagine a couple of months later Patty is on a date with Brian. Brian is a school teacher and their dates consist of fast food and long walks on the boardwalk. But Patty has deeply connected with Brian and fallen in love.

One night, Brian invites Patty out to a diner. In the midst of the crowded noisy diner, while sitting in a fully lit hardwood booth, Brian takes from his pocket a cheap jewelry box and places it in front of Patty. Patty's face lights up. She begins to shake and sweat. She nervously smiles from ear to ear.

Patty is immersed in the moment and oblivious to the customers in the booths around them who are watching. Patty is deeply touched even before she opens the jewelry box. Although the ring itself does not compare to the sapphire that Glenn tried to give her, to Patty, it's the most beautiful ring she ever received.

The most important thing about a present is that it embodies the presence of the one who gave it to you. When you get a gift from someone you love, you love it; not because of what it is, but because of who gave it to you.

One night I made a model of an ancient scroll with my son. We glued the ends of twenty pieces of paper together, colored the long sheet with pictures and letters, rolled it up, wrapped it with a ribbon, and cut a hole in a fancy bag and used it as a protective cover. The whole process took about forty-five minutes. The scroll looked homemade, but it lasted a lot longer than most of his store-bought toys. I had no other reason to make that scroll other than to be with my son—and he knew it. He felt my undivided presence. Any toy gift would have lasted a couple of days. But something we made together could have meaning forever. What our children need most are not our presents; it's our presence. They don't need toys. They need us. And Toys R *not* Us. We are the gift.

The *intimacy interview* will reveal hundreds of opportunities for you to give to your spouse. In every case, the most important thing to give is *you*. *You* have to be within your giving. Your spouse needs to be able to feel your presence in your presents. I can't offer you a formula to succeed with this matter. It's a function of intention. If it comes from your heart, it will go into your spouse's heart

I once heard a story about a man and woman on a blind date. From the moment they met, the man was talking about himself. He talked about his friends, his work, his travels, and his gym. He went on for hours, until finally he said, "That's enough about me. Let's talk about you. What do you think about me?"

Love can't be selfish. It can't be all about you. Giving to your spouse can't be about getting love for yourself. Love is the by-product, but your giving has to be unconditional. And the purest thing you can give is you.

It's easy to buy a gift. But the right gift, given at the

right time and in the right way—that takes time and energy. That's an art. It's not about money. The size of the gift makes no difference. It's the giving itself that makes the difference.

There are two sayings that couldn't be truer. One is "money can't buy you love." And the other is "it's the thought that counts." These sayings share a common message. The most important thing to give is your presence. No matter what you give, make sure *you* are in it. In the words of Ralph Waldo Emerson, "The only gift is a portion of thyself."

Love Conquers All

My wife and I have four children, all of whom were born prematurely. As is often the case with preemies, our babies had to spend a few weeks in the Neonatal Intensive Care Unit (NICU) at the hospital before we could bring them home. During the time when our babies were in the NICU, my wife and I visited the hospital everyday to help the nurses care for the babies. We fed them, changed their diapers, burped them, wrapped them tightly in blankets, assisted in the changing of their IV, and did whatever the nurses would permit us to do.

A hospital is not a nice place to spend every day for weeks, but we were committed to being with our babies because we yearned to bond with them, and we knew that bond wouldn't simply be waiting for us when the babies came home. We knew that if we wanted to connect with our babies, we would have to begin caring for them and giving to them immediately.

The care we provided for our babies while they were in the NICU helped us connect with them—it changed our experience of their time in the hospital. But what was particularly fascinating to us, which highlights the central theme of MARRIAGE FITNESS, is that giving to our babies changed *their* experience in the hospital too. The nurses explained (citing medical research) that the more parents of preemies care for their baby, the better it is for the baby's health. How could that be? Why does it matter who feeds the baby as long as the baby gets the nutrition it needs? Is the baby even aware of who changes its diaper? In the medical community, the research is indisputable, but the reason is a mystery. I'm not a doctor or a medical researcher, but I believe I can explain. It's simple. Nurses provide medical care. Parents *give presence*. Giving presence creates love. Love changes everything. Love conquers all.

Summary

Giving is usually something we do when we feel love. But the relationship between giving and love works the other way too. You will feel love for those to whom you give. So interview your spouse, collect an inventory of giving opportunities, and *give* to your spouse at least three times each day. And don't forget to give the most important thing—your presence.

The MarriageMax™ 4-Step Plan

1. Put Love First
2. Give Presence
3. **Move from Me to We**
4. Save Yourself

Chapter 6

MOVE FROM ME TO WE

There was one part of our wedding that was extraordinary. It's called the *bedekin*. The *bedekin* is an ancient ceremony performed at some Jewish weddings moments before the marriage ceremony. The *bedekin* symbolizes one of the keys to creating a lasting core connection and deep love. Allow me to explain.

When it was time for our *bedekin,* I was escorted by the rabbi and some of my friends to a room where most of the guests waited huddled around my wife. When we entered the room, everyone turned toward us. As I was escorted toward my wife, the guests parted one by one just before we converged. I couldn't see my wife, but as the people stepped aside, I knew I was getting closer and being escorted to where she was seated. Eventually, the last row of people surrounding my wife moved aside, and I saw her sitting in an ornate high-backed white chair fit for a queen, holding hands with my mother and my mother-in-law who sat on either side of her. I approached my wife and performed the ceremonial part of the *bedekin*—I took the veil that was over her head and lowered it so that it covered her face. I left the room and waited for my wife to join me under the marriage canopy.

The traditional explanation for the *bedekin* is that the groom is checking to make sure he is marrying the right woman and that he doesn't fall victim to a last minute switch as Jacob did in biblical times when he was tricked into marrying Leah instead of Rachel.

In the Bible, Jacob waited seven years to marry Rachel whom he loved. But on his wedding night he was duped into marrying Rachel's older sister, Leah. It wasn't until after his marriage to Leah that he married his true love, Rachel (in biblical times, polygamy was acceptable and common).

The problem with the traditional explanation of the *bedekin* is that it doesn't make sense or hold-up to scrutiny.

If the *bedekin* was my opportunity to ensure I was marrying the right woman, I wouldn't cover my bride's face; I would *uncover* it. Symbolically and practically, it makes more sense to lift the veil and reveal her identity than it does to cover her face and conceal it. But, in fact, tradition says to lower the veil and conceal her identity.

Furthermore, if the *bedekin* was my opportunity to confirm I was marrying the right woman and protect myself against being tricked, then after I lifted the veil and revealed her identify, I should immediately escort her to the marriage canopy—never letting her out of my sight. But that's not the tradition of the *bedekin*. I didn't escort her to the marriage canopy; I met her there. I separated from my bride for a few minutes after the *bedekin,* leaving myself completely vulnerable to a fate that I am supposedly protecting myself against. In the time that it took my bride to join me under the marriage canopy, another woman could have taken her place and her identity would have been concealed by the veil.

In spite of the traditional explanation, the *bedekin* does not protect a man from marrying the wrong woman, nor does it symbolically represent that message.

The traditional explanation seems implausible for another reason too. Is it possible that Jacob could be tricked into marrying the wrong woman? It's not as if Rachel and Leah were identical twins. Rachel was known to be a shapely and beautiful woman. Leah is described as having weak eyes. Did Jacob really not know who he was marrying? Is it possible that he couldn't tell the difference until the next morning as the verses indicate?

A careful reading of the story reveals a more reasonable and insightful understanding of Jacob and the true meaning of the *bedekin*.

On the day after his wedding, Jacob asked why he was not given Rachel to marry. He doesn't ask why he *was* given Leah. In other words, Jacob didn't complain that he married Leah. He complained that he didn't marry Rachel. Why didn't he complain about marrying Leah? Would you accept a marriage to someone you had no intention of marrying without putting up a fuss?

Jacob was told two things when he asked why he wasn't given Rachel to marry. He was told that the custom in his community was for the older sister to marry first (Leah was the older sister). And he was told that he would marry Rachel too. Jacob accepted this response without argument, and, in fact, he married Rachel too.

But why did this response satisfy Jacob? If you discovered that you married the wrong woman, would you accept your fate because of a local custom?

The response satisfied Jacob, but not because he learned that the local custom mandated he marry Leah. The response satisfied Jacob because he learned that he was going to marry Rachel. Let me explain.

Jacob lived in the community as a single man for seven years. He knew the custom was that the older sister marries first. That's why he didn't complain about marrying Leah. Can you imagine being a single man living in a community with such a custom and not knowing it? Jacob knew he had to marry Leah—that wasn't a problem for him. He *wanted* to marry Rachel, and the fact that he did not—that was a problem for him. So when he was told that he would marry Rachel, he was satisfied. That's all he wanted. He didn't need an explanation for why he married Leah. He knew he had to marry Leah *in order* to marry Rachel. He knew that to marry the woman of his choice, he had to marry the woman of his fate too. And that's why the story of Jacob serves as a paragon for a successful marriage. Because the truth is when you marry, you marry Rachel and Leah. You choose your spouse, but that choice includes the future of your spouse which you don't yet know—your fate. And to succeed in love, you have to commit to both—Rachel *and* Leah, your choice *and* your fate, the revealed *and* the unrevealed.

So what's the meaning of the *bedekin?*

The *bedekin* is a vow of unconditional love. I lowered the veil to hide my wife's face, signifying our unqualified commitment to each other—a commitment that included everything we knew and chose about each other *and* everything hidden from each other that we would only discover in the future.

Most people don't enter a marriage with this attitude. Most people, when they wake up to find Leah lying next to them, complain that Leah was not their choice. Most people become frustrated with their spouse and their marriage when they discover character flaws, problems, and differences. Most people feel so duped into marrying Leah that they divorce Rachel. But it's not possible to marry one without the other. Leah always appears. The key to success in love and marriage is to know what to do when "she" does.

Soul mates are not perfect for each other. Soul mates love each other with all their imperfections. Soul mates love each other no matter what. Step three of the MarriageMax™ 4-Step Plan for connecting your cores and building love is to embrace your spouse's shortcomings, uniqueness, and challenges. Step three is to *move from me to we.*

Take Interest in Your Spouse's Interests

Your fate includes your spouse's ever-changing interests. When you met, you shared some of your spouse's interests. And the interests you didn't share, at least you knew what they were. But people's interests change over time. However, change is not, in and of itself, a threat to your marriage.

It's how you *react* to your spouse's changing interests that determines whether you grow apart or stay connected.

Sometimes I hear about marriages between celebrities. One spouse is filming for six months in Europe while the other is touring the United States. They talk to each other through the tabloids and plan to spend the holidays together at the end of the year. A Hollywood love affair seems exciting, but like two stars in the sky, there is too much distance between them. They aren't connected.

A Hollywood marriage is an extreme example, but some couples live separate lives even when they sleep under one roof. Some couples have separate hobbies, friends, careers, exercise routines, and chores. Their lives parallel each other—they may even be well coordinated—but they do not intersect. *And if your lives don't intersect, you will not connect.*

This is why we're amazed to learn about some couples who split up. Everything seemed fine in their life. In fact, they functioned at a high level. Everything was in order. They succeeded in their job and got along with their family and friends. But they had no connection between them. They had an interesting and active life, but they didn't share it.

I knew a man who changed careers to pursue his dream. His work wasn't only how he earned a living, it became his mission in life. But his wife didn't care about his mission. All she cared about were the practical ramifications of his job: his work schedule, travel schedule, and income. His passion for his mission and his wife's lack of involvement in it made it difficult for them to connect with each other.

That same man's wife became passionate about gardening. She spent a lot of time in her garden—planting, pruning, and weeding. She also read gardening magazines and talked in Internet chat rooms with other gardeners. Unfortunately, her husband wanted nothing to do with *her* garden, so once again, they grew apart.

There are many ways you can grow apart emotionally from your spouse. Sometimes it's not one area but an overall lack of interest and involvement in each other's mundane

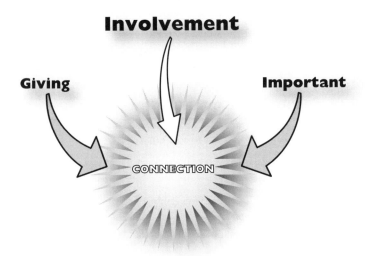

lives that creates the split. In either case, lack of involvement is tantamount to a lack of connection.

Falling in love is the opposite experience. In the beginning of a relationship, it's natural to be interested in each other. Couples talk for hours about each other's hobbies. They watch each other play sports. They exercise together. They visit each other at work. They meet each other's friends and family. They go to each other's favorite restaurant. They watch each other's favorite movie. They help each other with projects. They look through each other's photo albums and ask about each other's collectibles. When a couple falls in love, their lives intertwine.

Soul mates get involved with each other. They talk about almost everything. They do lots of things together—and everything is fun. This doesn't mean soul mates necessarily share the same interests. My wife had no interest in basketball, but she still came to watch me play. Soul mates get involved with each other not because they're compatible, but because they want to be soul mates. *Involvement with your spouse will create a connection between you and your spouse.*

Consider how you took interest in your spouse's life in the beginning of your relationship. Do you remember getting involved with and learning about your spouse's friends, family, profession, interests, and hobbies? Do you see how moving from "me" to "we" helped to create love between you? Do you see how taking an interest in your spouse created a connection between you?

Are you still active in your spouse's life? Did "Leah" appear with any new interests? If so, how did you react? Does your spouse have a new job, passion, hobby, or group of friends? Did you get involved with the new aspects of your spouse's life? Did you embrace your fate or reject it?

One way to *move from me to we* is to get involved in as many aspects of your spouse's life as possible. Don't let "Leah" be a stranger. *You and your spouse don't have to be interested in the same things to be soul mates—you only have to be interested in each other.*

Every new aspect of your lives—every friend, every interest, every hobby, every meeting, every diet, every fitness program, every project, every trip, every phone call—is an opportunity to *move from me to we.* Are you living separate lives or building love together? Have you embraced your fate or is Leah estranged? Did you ask about your spouse's sales meeting? Did you go together to pick out the new outfit? Do you jog together or workout separately? Did you shop for the new couch together? You and your spouse have a fixed amount of hours, people, meetings, activities, and meals in your life. How much of it you share and how you share it determines the depth of your connection.

Everything is an opportunity to connect with your spouse. As easily as gardening can divide a couple, it can unite a couple. There is nothing inherently divisive about any hobby or interest. Your marriage is impacted not by the hobbies you choose, but by whether or not you take an interest in each other's selections.

When you were single and you planned a vacation, the only thing that mattered was the plans you made—and *you* made them. But in your marriage, your plans are secondary to the planning. It's your involvement with each other that matters most. If you plan the vacation together—if it's a "we" experience—you'll have a great time and be in the right place. If you make the plans alone, the pictures may not tell the whole story.

Imagine you and your spouse's life as two circles. The degree to which you overlap your circles determines the depth of your connection. Soul mates overlap a lot. Soul mates are constantly involved in some way in almost every aspect of each other's life. That doesn't mean soul mates do everything together. That's impossible. And it doesn't mean that their involvement is extensive in all cases. That's impossible too. However, soul mates are part of many aspects of each other's lives in some way. They ask about each other's lives, talk about each other's lives, review each other's drafts, buy things together, shop for things together, research things together, exercise together, read some of the same magazines and books, work on projects together, and play together. Their involvement with each facilitates their connection to each other.

I am credited as the author of this book, but the truth is I have a co-author—my wife. My wife wasn't interested in writing a book on marriage success and revealing how we transformed our marriage, but she took an interest because it was my passion. We discussed every part of the book. She read every draft. We spent hours brainstorming about the title and subtitle. We spent an evening in a book store looking at book covers and discussing cover design. But the most important thing about her involvement was not that it made the book better (although it certainly did), but that it made us better. We created the book, but creating it helped to create our love.

To *move from me to we* is not only about getting involved with each other; it's about being intimate. It's possible to be involved with your spouse but not be connected. The goal is to connect. The most important part of the *move from me to we* is not the change in your schedule and interests; it's the change in you. When "you" become "we," then you've made the move.

Getting involved with your spouse is how you get to

know your spouse's thoughts, feelings, dreams, fears, and opinions. Try to appreciate your spouse's interests from their perspective. What need does it satisfy for your spouse? What dream does it fulfill? Try to learn as much as you can about your spouse's inner life as well as the world of their hobbies and interests.

Move Your Circle of Life (Exercise 3.1)

To *move from me to we* requires a consistent consciousness—it's a lifestyle. There is no specific discipline that guarantees success. However, the correct consciousness without a discipline is also likely to fail. Therefore, I want to offer exercises to help you *move from me to we.*

Move your circle of life is designed to transform one of your spouse's interests that caused you to grow apart into one that brings you together.

If a man was attracted to his wife partly because she wanted to be a homemaker, their marriage will be challenged when she decides to open an art gallery and work full-time even though they have four children. Unwelcome interests are objectively neutral but can be a problem from one spouse's perspective. They can easily cause a couple to grow apart.

Make a list of the interests and activities that have become a significant part of your spouse's life since you fell in love.

1. _____
2. _____
3. _____
4. _____
5. _____
6. _____
7. _____
8. _____

Circle the ones with which you're least involved and the ones that most interfere with your marriage. Choose one you circled that offers the best and most realistic opportunity for you to get involved.

Getting involved does not necessarily mean that you have to do the activity together. It could mean that you watch the activity, plan for it, pack for it, budget for it, buy supplies for it, or research it in preparation for discussion. How you get involved depends on you, your spouse, and the interest. There are endless possibilities. The goal is to *move your circle of life* so that it overlaps with your spouse's interest.

Choose an interest that is important to your spouse. The more important it is to your spouse, the greater the impact your involvement will have on your marriage. If your spouse jogs one hour every day, that's a better choice than science fiction if your spouse reads only one science fiction book each year.

Move your circle of life is intended to increase "we" in your marriage. Don't choose an interest that is already part of your "we." If you wanted to strengthen a weak muscle, you would add a new exercise to your physical fitness routine. Choose something that is interfering with your marriage. Choose something that will impact your marriage when you get involved.

Consider your interest in the topic when you make your selection. Your spouse's passion for the interest is more important, but if you're trying to decide between two interests that are of equal importance to your spouse, choose the one that interests you more. The more interest you have in the topic, the easier it will be for you to get involved.

After you choose one of your spouse's interests, be cautious about how you involve yourself. Don't show up unexpectedly at your spouse's weekly card game. Begin by reading about the subject and educating yourself. Then engage your spouse in discussion about the topic. Ask questions. Show your interest. Consider purchasing a thoughtful gift that relates to your spouse's interest. In time, explore with your spouse how you can get more involved. Be assertive, but make sure you involve yourself in ways that are agreeable to your spouse.

The chances are good that your spouse's interest doesn't interest you. If it did, you would probably already be involved. *Move your circle of life* is challenging in that regard. It takes discipline. *Move your circle of life* is not an exercise in choosing compatibility; it's an exercise in choosing love. Your interest in your spouse's interest is irrelevant. Your interest in love is the key.

Consider a father whose son developed a passion for baseball. One summer he took his son to see every major league team play one game. Their travels took the entire summer and cost a lot of money, but it did wonders for their relationship.

Upon their return the father was asked, "Do you like baseball that much?"

"No," he replied. "But I like my son that much."

Ironically, however, the more you get involved in your spouse's interest, the more fun it will be. I know it's hard to imagine. I know you have zero interest in bass fishing. But if your interest in love is genuine, anything can be a source of your connection. And once you connect, everything is fun. Love is all that matters. If you can create love, you'll be happy doing anything together.

My son became interested in tennis when he was four- years-old. Occasionally we played together at the public courts. Anyone watching might have felt sorry for me having to chase the ball all over the court (and over the fence). But I had a great time. Did I sign up to be the four-year-old tennis coach? No. But I would play with my son anytime. Tennis (or any activity) can be fun or boring, fulfilling or meaningless. It depends on the depth of your connection with the person with whom you're involved.

Move your circle of life is an opportunity for personal growth too. Think of your spouse's interest as your new hobby and consider your spouse your in-house tutor. Take advantage of the situation. View it as an opportunity to expand yourself and your knowledge of the world. Solicit your spouse's thoughts, opinions, and advice on the topic.

My wife would not have known the first thing about writing and publishing a book if she didn't take an interest in my passion. Now she could publish one herself. That's one of the benefits of love. You become more than you were alone—more knowledgeable, more interesting, more experienced, more worldly. True love is self expanding.

Pick a Hobby—any Hobby (Exercise 3.2)

Getting involved in new areas of your spouse's life is not easy. You're probably already involved in the areas of your spouse's life that interest you. And the areas that don't interest you—that's probably why you're not involved. I hope that will change when you *move your circle of life* and utilize the wisdom of this chapter. But if it's involvement with each other that creates love, let me also suggest an easy way.

Talk with your spouse about a new hobby that you can do together. *Pick a hobby—any hobby.* It can be anything you and your spouse wish. Here are a few ideas: investing, Thai massage, cooking, tennis, square dancing, poetry, dried flowers, body-painting, acupuncture, gardening, wine tasting, antiques, Bible study, karaoke, bird watching, fly-fishing, baking, photography, rollerblading, bicycling, stamp collecting, and astronomy.

Make sure the hobby you select is a shared interest. It should be something fun for both of you. *Move your circle of life* can be challenging. *Pick a hobby—any hobby* should be easy.

Once you select your hobby, get into it. Search the Internet, send away for information, visit the local library, join an association, sign up for a newsletter, register for a seminar, enroll in a class, visit a bookstore, talk to experts, and do it. There is only one rule—you have to do it together!

Your new hobby can be a great topic for your *talk*

charges and *super talk charges*. It can be a great idea for *date night*. It can be a theme for a *romantic retreat*. There are also so many creative ways to *give* to your spouse when you have a shared interest. Once you pick a hobby, see how well you can incorporate it into the other exercises suggested in MARRIAGE FITNESS.

My wife and I recently picked reading as our hobby. There was an intriguing self-help book that we both wanted to read, so we decided to read it together. My wife reads aloud, I listen, and we talk about the author's point whenever we feel inspired.

Sometimes we read for a few minutes. Sometimes we read for a couple of hours. Sometimes we take the book to Starbucks and presto—*date night*. If it's time for a *super talk charge,* we can always count on reading the book aloud to stimulate an intimate dialogue.

For us, reading a self-help book is a great hobby to share because not only do we connect by being together, but also through the richness of our discussions.

You might consider reading as your hobby too. Instead of self-help, maybe you want to read love poems, mystery novels, or classic literature. How about reading MARRIAGE FITNESS together?

Make Room for Love (Exercise 3.3)

Consider a husband who is obsessed with a computer game. Every night he comes home from work and invests his final waking hours and emotional energy into beating his top score. Can you imagine how annoyed his wife is losing the battle for his attention night after night to a computer game? To make matters worse, he occasionally demands her attention at midnight when she's exhausted. Sometimes the challenge is not for one spouse to get involved with the other's interest, but for the other spouse to drop the interest for the benefit of the marriage.

If you and your spouse implement *move your circle of life* and *pick a hobby—any hobby,* you will share some new interests. But if you are like most couples, you have built an extensive life exclusive of your spouse. There are probably still interests and activities that contribute to your "me" and detract from your "we." What are those interests? To what extent are they outside the context of your marriage? How often and for how long do they separate you from each other? To what extent do they disconnect you emotionally?

The last two exercises accomplish a *move from me to we* by increasing "we." *Make room for love* accomplishes it by decreasing "me."

List *your* interests and hobbies that most detract from your marriage.

1. _____

2. _____

3. _____

4. _____

5. _____

6. _____

7. _____

8. _____

Select one interest or hobby that detracts from your "we" and try to live without it. Do you have a favorite TV show that doesn't interest your spouse? Don't watch it anymore. Do you go away with a friend for a three-day golf outing every year? Don't go this year. Do you play in a bowling league every Wednesday night? Plan to spend the time at home instead. Search your life for something that interferes with your marriage and try to live without it. Limit "me" and make room in your circle of life for more "we."

Be careful not to pick something that will make you bitter, but also try to pick something that will have a meaningful impact on your marriage.

It's hard to trade "me" for "we," but *your* life ended when your marriage began. Now it's time for "we"—and for that you need to make room. Some couples don't connect because their lives outside the context of their marriage are too big. There's simply no time and energy for another person. Cut something out. Make space for your spouse. In the end, you'll lose a hobby, but you'll gain love. It's one of the best trades you will ever make.

Consider your selection carefully. If poker is your passion, it might be better for your spouse to try to get involved with your poker game rather than you eliminating it from your life. On the other hand, if poker is not important to you and your spouse is not involved in it, then maybe it is a good choice.

I'm not suggesting that you and your spouse should never spend time away from each other. Everyone needs private time, and it's also reasonable to have interests that don't involve your spouse. The goal here is to remove an interest that interferes with your marriage. It's a judgment call—one you might consider making together.

I appreciated my wife's interest in my basketball game, but I don't play anymore. It took too much time, and except for watching an occasional game, it was difficult for my wife to be involved. It's still important to me to be physically fit, so I speed-walk on the treadmill at home. It takes less time, and we can talk while I'm exercising, or I do it early in the morning before anyone in the house wakes up. I miss playing basketball, but it was not worth the time and energy it took from my marriage.

"My Wife's Leg Hurts *Us*"

Your spouse's character flaws, problems, and misfortunes are part of your fate too. When your spouse's neatness turns out to be a compulsive neurotic disorder, your marriage has a problem. When your spouse is diagnosed with a life-threatening illness, your love will be tested. The secret to handling these types of discoveries successfully is to *move from me to we*.

As a child and teenager, your primary concern was yourself. You probably got twenty years practice being selfish. When you were a baby, you cried until you were fed. You didn't care if it was 3 a.m. and your mom was asleep or 2 p.m. and she was on an important phone call. All you cared about was satisfying your hunger.

When mothers nurse, it's important they get enough calcium in their diet. It's not important for their baby; it's important for *them*. Their baby will get enough calcium regardless. The question is whether it will come from their mother's diet or from her teeth. Either way, the baby will take it. Babies only know "me."

Most of us become big babies. Some people are so selfish, they only love their dogs because they can train them to obey their command. But selfish people are always disappointed in marriage because people can't be trained. They're unpredictable. Dormant problems get revealed and misfortune strikes. "Leah" always appears. Selfishness can get you most of what you want except what you need most— love. Love requires a new state-of-mind. Love requires a *move from me to we.*

To change the word "me" to "we," you flip the "m"— turn it upside down. True love requires you to change your perspective 180 degrees. Not only are your problems your problem, but your spouse's problems become your problem too. Sometimes that means your life gets turned upside down.

True love is unconditional. When you and your spouse discover your differences, flaws, and problems, that's not when your marriage ends; it's when you *move from me to we* and build lasting love. Of course you didn't expect him to have a fierce temper. I know you didn't know she was sexually abused by her stepdad. No one wanted him to have a stroke. But for a marriage to succeed, you have to commit to Rachel *and* Leah. You have to accept your choice *and* your fate. This is the art of loving—making a space in your life for the entirety of another person.

It's easy to embrace your spouse's good attributes and joy in life. But that's not love; it's compatibility. You can't love some of your spouse. True love is inclusive of flaws, differences, and tragedy. True love includes your fate as well as your choice.

I know a man who discovered after ten years of marriage that his wife was an alcoholic. At first, he was angry. But later he shared with me that it was the turning point in their marriage. After he got over the initial shock and disappointment, he supported his wife in her battle. The more he showed his support, the more she revealed about her inner struggle, and the more intimate they became. It was an extremely challenging ordeal, but one that deeply connected them.

Love is like a hug. You can't hug a piece of your spouse. You have to open your arms and let in the whole person. When you hug, there is no space between you. You are completely connected. If you want to sculpt two people hugging, you begin with one block of clay, not two. Love is a process of two people becoming one.

A husband takes his wife to the doctor to have her leg examined. When it was her turn to see the doctor, they went in together. The doctor asked what was wrong. The husband responds, "My wife's leg hurts *us*." To succeed in a marriage, you have to live with your spouse's flaws just as you live with your own. In love—in "we"—your spouse's flaws *are* your own. People say "love is blind." *True love is not blind. True love is seeing and still loving.*

You don't have to like your spouse's flaws. I'm sure you don't like your own. As discussed in Chapter 2, you can work together to change them. But the key to creating love is not changing them; it's embracing them. Changing them will improve your compatibility, which is not a bad thing, but embracing them will create love—that's the most important thing.

I used to feel that my wife's flaws were compromising the quality of my life. Certain things were a disappointment to me. But then I realized that my life was being compromised not by her flaws, but by my attitude. To *move from me to we* and embrace the frailties of my wife was not self-limiting; it was self-expanding. The more problems I embraced, the more we connected. Ironically, problems that seem to inhibit love can create a connection that produces love. What a wonderful way to think of your spouse's problems—as an opportunity to connect and create love.

A good marriage is a team. The issue is not who is at fault. The issue is how *we* can solve the problem. Consider you and your spouse a team and your problems as your opponent. Look for solutions, not blame. Use your problems to unite you, not divide you.

What flaws and problems have been revealed by your spouse? How did you react to discovering them? Are you on the same team trying to solve them? Or do you blame your spouse for them? Do you think you have embraced your fate or are you fighting to reject it?

The following insight may help you embrace your spouse's flaws. Everyone has their blessings and curses. In most cases, both stem from the same personality trait. For example, my wife appreciates my emotional strength and clarity of thought. She's challenged by my stubbornness. Both the blessing and the curse, however, originate from the same attribute.

Think about this in the context of your marriage. What do you love most about your spouse? What do you dislike most about your spouse? Does your like and dislike originate from the same quality? Do you see how your spouse is a package deal? You can't change what you don't like without changing what you do like. Rachel and Leah are the same person. You can't marry one without marrying the other too.

Imagine you and your spouse are two different color translucent strips. If you put your strips on top of one another, you get a third color. That's what it means to *move from me to we*. It's a big change, but it's not a compromise or sacrifice. The new color still includes one hundred percent of your original color—and much more. You've expanded. You have new interests, problems, insights, hobbies, attributes—and, most importantly, you have love.

Be a Team (Exercise 3.4)

Make a list of *your* problems and flaws.

1. _____
2. _____
3. _____
4. _____
5. _____
6. _____

7. _____

8. _____

9. _____

10. _____

Circle the one your spouse accepts the least. Place a check-mark next to the one your spouse criticizes or attacks you for the most. You may circle and check-mark the same one. Choose the one you circled or the one you check-marked and invite your spouse to help you solve that problem.

Use a *date night,* a *romantic retreat,* or a *super talk charge* to share with your spouse the details of your problem. Try to describe the root of your struggle. Talk about your child-hood, a life-changing incident, an accident, a tragedy, or medical details if they are relevant. Share your thoughts, feelings, fears, and insights regarding your struggle. Allow yourself to be vulnerable. Reveal your inner life. And finally, invite your spouse to battle your problem with you. Tell your spouse how to help. Be as specific as possible. The more involved your spouse gets, the more you will connect, and the more love there will be in your life.

Invest together in solving your problem. Read about it, research it, talk to experts, consult with therapists or medical doctors, talk with others who have the same struggle, and surf the Internet for information.

The goal of *be a team* is not to solve the problem (although I hope you do). The goal is to transform the problem from one that divides you into one that unites you. In a marriage, problems are not a problem. They are neutral. They can either destroy love or create love. It depends on how you and your spouse handle them. If you're on the same team, you can live with anything. If you're not, the slightest problem will drive you nuts.

I am purposely not discussing how you and your spouse should solve your problem. That's an important dis-cussion, but it doesn't belong in this book. This book is about how to create love. I'm sure there are other books about how to solve your problem (and you should read them *together*). But to create love, you don't have to solve your problem; you only have to attack it together. Teamwork creates love.

How to Make Decisions

Business owners often ask their employees for their opinions regarding certain decisions. Why? The boss probably has the most experience and information with which to base the decision. The boss probably doesn't need advice. Why do business owners take the time and energy to include their employees in certain decisions?

A good business owner asks their employees for their opinion not only to seek insight, but to increase team spirit too. As employee involvement increases, so does employee commitment. Involvement creates connection. Tell someone what to do and they feel like an employee. Ask their opinion and they feel like a partner.

A smart business owner also lets their employees influence their decision regardless of the quality of their advice. It's easy to utilize advice when it's helpful. But a wise business owner knows how to utilize employee advice not only for its quality, but for the impact utilizing it has on the employee. The more an employee influences their company, the more they connect to it.

If employees are recommending a decision that will cause the company to lose twenty percent of its business, obviously the boss needs to exercise his authority. However, many business decisions are not critical. When a company decides about suppliers, health plans, office décor, retreat location, advertising mediums, and computer brands, the opportunity to involve employees may be more important than making the "right" decision. In fact, the right decision may be the one an employee recommends—not because it's the optimal choice, but because the impact on employee morale outweighs the fact that there was a better choice.

Move from Me to We Marriage Assessment

List below nine decisions YOU are responsible for on a regular basis. For example: vacations, family diet, children's schooling, children's play dates, investments, insurance coverage, entertainment plans, holiday plans, and work related decisions.

    Next to each decision, rank the extent to which you include your spouse in those decisions based on the following scale.

0 – don't include at all
1 – include a little
2 – include a lot

Add your score and measure it against the scale below.

Decisions	**Ranking**
1.	
2.	
3.	
4.	
5.	
6.	
7.	

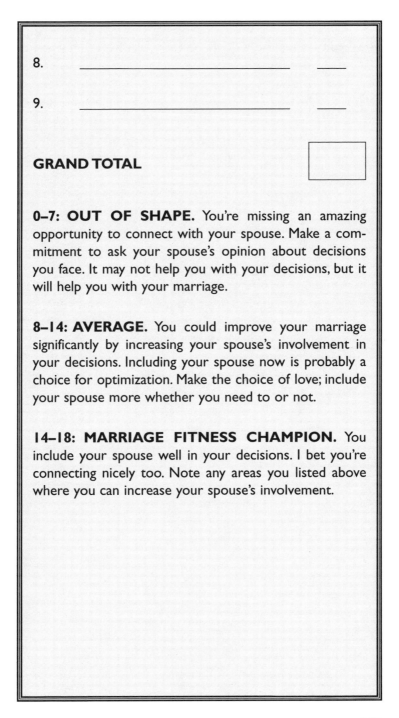

8. _____ ____

9. _____ ____

GRAND TOTAL

0–7: OUT OF SHAPE. You're missing an amazing opportunity to connect with your spouse. Make a commitment to ask your spouse's opinion about decisions you face. It may not help you with your decisions, but it will help you with your marriage.

8–14: AVERAGE. You could improve your marriage significantly by increasing your spouse's involvement in your decisions. Including your spouse now is probably a choice for optimization. Make the choice of love; include your spouse more whether you need to or not.

14–18: MARRIAGE FITNESS CHAMPION. You include your spouse well in your decisions. I bet you're connecting nicely too. Note any areas you listed above where you can increase your spouse's involvement.

One way to facilitate your *move from me to we* is to involve your spouse in your decisions. Solicit your spouse's opinion—and utilize it whenever possible. Let your spouse influence you. Make decisions together. The point is not necessarily to arrive at a better decision. The point is to get intimately involved in each other's life, to connect, and to create love.

A good marriage requires spouses to have their roles. You may be responsible for planning the family vacations while your spouse makes the investment decisions. It's healthy to have division of responsibility. However, it's not healthy to exclude each other from the areas for which you're responsible. You may not need your spouse to make your decisions. But you need your spouse for love. Love comes from making decisions together.

Making decisions together does not mean you have an equal say. Many areas of your life will have a final decision maker. If you work in investments, then you should probably make the final investment decisions. But you should discuss the investments with your spouse. It doesn't matter if your spouse knows the difference between a stock and a bond. It's not the advice that's important; it's your connection.

A long time ago I visited a condominium apartment I considered buying. On my way in, I met a man who was on his way out. I asked him what he thought of the apartment. He said the shower had great water pressure and that his wife was looking at the rest of the apartment. He boasted that the water pressure was all he cared about. I remember being impressed with their compatibility. I imagined him saying to his wife, "Whatever you want, honey."

I realize now that that couple may have been compatible, but they were also disconnected. I'm sure his wife got the apartment she wanted, but I don't think she had the marriage she wanted.

To what extent do you and your spouse include each other in decisions? Do you seek each other's advice?

I once worked with someone who never made a significant business decision without consulting with his wife. His wife had no official position in the business, nor did she know much about it. But he wouldn't make a decision until he spoke with her. They were partners—not simply in business—but in life.

The best decision you can make is the one that results in love. For love you don't have to decide correctly; you have to decide together. It's usually better to make the wrong decision together than to make the right decision alone. If you have love, you can live with any decision. If you're disconnected from each other, nothing will be right anyway.

Some couples are disconnected because they divide responsibilities and don't involve each other in their areas. Other couples have the opposite problem—they fight about every decision.

Some people are so concerned about getting their way that they destroy their marriage in the process. Did you ever go to bed angry because your spouse wouldn't watch the program you wanted? Or both of you watched what you wanted but in separate rooms? If you got your way but disconnected from your spouse, you won the battle and lost the war.

There is nothing more important than your connection to your spouse. If you fight about a decision and win, you may end up making the right decision, but doing the wrong thing. You never know how a decision will turn out. You may think you're right, but it may turn out wrong. You can't control the outcome of your decisions. But you can control the love you create when deciding. And that will determine the outcome of your life. Making the right decision is unpredictable. Making love is a sure thing. "Make love" by making decisions together.

What Do You Think? (Exercise 3.5)

Pick one area of your life in which you make decisions regularly without consulting your spouse. Involve your spouse in those decisions and let your spouse influence the outcome.

The purpose of this exercise is to help you form a new habit that will eventually impact all the areas of your life in which you make decisions. Therefore, choose an area you make decisions frequently. If you make investment decisions once a year, investments are not a good choice. If you're responsible for the food shopping, then decisions about the family diet might be a good idea.

I have a friend who is a high-powered entrepreneur. His work is very stressful and he has a lot of money at stake everyday. He prides himself on never bringing his work home with him. He refuses to discuss anything about his business with his wife, and he insists that this is the best approach for his marriage. But it's not.

He leaves his work at the office, but not his stress. And his wife has no idea what's going on in his head. She feels excluded from a major part of his life. She knows she can't help, but her wish to be included is not for practical purposes. She just wants to connect to him.

It would be so easy for him to share some of what is going on at work and to even ask her opinion about some of his outstanding issues. She may not solve his business problems, but including her would solve one of their marriage problems.

Summary

When you marry, you choose your spouse, but that choice includes the future of your spouse which you don't yet know—your fate. And to succeed in love, you have to commit to both—Rachel *and* Leah, your choice *and* your fate, the revealed *and* the unrevealed.

Step three of the MarriageMax™ 4-Step Plan for connecting your cores and building phenomenal love is to embrace your spouse's shortcomings, uniqueness, and challenges. Step three is to *move from me to we*—to get involved in each other's lives. Here are five ways to *move from me to we*.

1. *Move your circle of life.* Get more involved in one of your spouse's hobbies or interests.

2. *Pick a hobby—any hobby.* You and your spouse select a hobby to do together.

3. *Make room for love.* Select one of your hobbies or interests that your spouse is not involved with and eliminate it from your life.

4. *Be a team.* Invite your spouse to help you fix one of your problems or flaws.

5. *What do you think?* Ask your spouse their opinion before making decisions.

"How to Forgive and be Forgiven"

FREE Online Supplement
Available now at www.Marriagemax.com/forgive.asp

The MarriageMax™ 4-Step Plan

1. Put Love First
2. Give Presence
3. Move from Me to We
4. **Save Yourself**

Chapter 7

SAVE YOURSELF

I once heard a violinist perform on a New York City subway. It was obvious he had many years of experience and training. His fingers changed positions lightning fast and the bow raced up and down the strings at every possible angle. He even knew how to tap the base of the violin to produce drum-like sounds. His passion and talent caused me to wonder why he was playing on a subway and not in a concert hall. But then the music started to bother me, and I realized why he was a street performer and not a professional. There was something critical missing from his music. He could make almost any sound with his violin, but there was one thing his energetic performance lacked—silence. He could play any note, but he couldn't seem to pause between notes. His performance was like a musical run-on sentence.

Great music is not simply sound; it's a combination of silence and sound. A master musician knows not only when to play, but when to pause.

Everything in life requires a balance between "silence" and "sound." In other words, you have to know what to do and what to refrain from doing. A friend has to know when to offer advice and when to just listen. A business owner has to know when to invest and when to say "no." A writer has to know what to say and what to leave to the reader's imagination. Parents have to know when to get involved and when to back-off.

153

A healthy society requires the same balance. Every citizen has both responsibilities and prohibitions. We have to pay taxes, dispose of our garbage, and properly care for our children. We are *not* permitted to steal, speed, or cause bodily harm to others.

Your marriage requires the same balance. To create a phenomenal marriage, you need to do certain things—*put love first, give presence, and move from me to we.* But you also need to refrain from doing certain things. *True love is a combination of initiating certain actions and ceasing from other actions.* Step four of the MarriageMax™ 4-Step Plan teaches you how to refrain from doing things that could interfere with your connection to your spouse. Step four of the MarriageMax™ 4-Step Plan is to *save yourself.*

Clear Your Cache

In most cases, couples lack true love not only because they don't do what is necessary to connect, but also because they do things they shouldn't which impede them from connecting. For example, if you're having an affair, besides the traumatic effect of betrayal, you can't connect with your spouse. It doesn't matter if your spouse is aware of the affair or not. The problem is not only your spouse's feelings. The problem is your ability to connect with your spouse. If you connect with someone else, then your soul is not available.

An affair is an obvious example, but there are many things that prevent couples from connecting. Playing a computer game obsessively can be the culprit. Your relationship with your mother could be the problem. Anything or anyone you let deep inside you can crowd out your spouse. *A soul can only have one mate.*

Consider a married salesman who was prospecting a huge account managed by a woman. In an effort to win her business, he began to cultivate a relationship with her. He took her out to lunch and asked her about her business as well as her personal interests. He discovered that she read books on spirituality. Whenever he saw related book reviews, he clipped it and mailed it with a nice note. He phoned her regularly for business and always asked about the book she was reading. Once he learned the title, he bought the book and read it too. He emailed her questions about the author's point and she happily offered her opinion. She referred him to other books, and he took her advice and read them too. Eventually, she gave him her business and their professional interaction created even more opportunity for them to connect personally.

Over time, genuine warmth developed between them. Instead of a handshake, they greeted each other with a hug and kiss on the cheek. On her birthday, he subscribed her to a spirituality book club. They talked and emailed about their personal lives in addition to their professional correspondence. When he had an argument with his boss, he called her to vent. When she had a bad date, she complained to him. The further their relationship developed, the more their lives intertwined personally and professionally.

Although their relationship was not sexual, their friendship satisfied many of his needs for intimacy. He felt an exciting energy whenever they touched, hugged, or kissed. He put a lot of thought into every email he sent her, and he checked his email in-box frequently in anticipation of her reply. He felt close to her. She became important in his life. They were always in touch. They shared time, interests, meals, emails, opinions, and some physical contact. They made a connection.

Since their relationship was professionally based, he thought it was appropriate and convinced himself that it didn't interfere with his marriage.

His wife knew about the relationship and it disturbed her. But what could she say? It was business. They were just friends. She had opposite sex friends too. But every time he climbed into bed with a book about spirituality, she felt he was going to bed with another woman. In fact, he seemed to lose interest in her sexually. And they never talked about the problems he had with his boss anymore. Something changed.

She didn't have the same role in his life anymore. She felt displaced.

You don't have to have sex to be unfaithful. Emotional infidelity damages marriages too. *The commitment to sleep with one person only guarantees you monogamy. The commitment to be with one person is what you need to create a phenomenal marriage.*

The chances are good that you already connect using some of the steps and exercises suggested in this book—but with someone other than your spouse! Who do you talk to the most during the day? Is there someone you spend quality time with each week? Is there someone you find yourself touching or kissing regularly? Is there someone to whom you send thoughtful emails, gifts, or media clippings? Do you go on vacation with someone other than your spouse? Do you share a common interest with someone? Do you solicit someone's opinion regularly? Or do you invest yourself in work or a hobby and connect with it?

There are universal principles which determine how to make a connection with someone or something. They work regardless of where you employ them. If you employ them with your spouse, you create love in your marriage. If you employ them elsewhere, you will create a connection that will interfere with your marriage. The principles are fixed. Where you apply them is up to you.

I'm not suggesting you shouldn't be committed to your work and have other relationships. There's no problem with either. But there's a big difference between being committed to your work and being connected to it. There's a big difference between having healthy relationships and having other soul mates. To create phenomenal love, you don't have to isolate yourself, but you do have to *save yourself.* True love is a result of a soul connection, and that can only happen if your soul is available.

You can't share your soul and still have true love with your spouse. Love is soul*full.* Like most awesome things in life, it's all-encompassing. Love is like a giant computer program—if you want to open it, you need your entire RAM available. For phenomenal love, you have to clear your cache.

You have many emotional needs including the need to connect. If you satisfy those needs outside your marriage, you won't satisfy them with your spouse. If you connect with someone or something else, your spouse will find you emotionally bankrupt. It's not that you *are* emotionally bankrupt; it's that you spent your soul elsewhere. The key to love is to remain available to your spouse. You have to *save yourself*. Don't let anyone else get to your soul. Spend it wisely. Spend it on love. Spend it on your spouse.

Next time you're upset and need to talk, don't call your sister. Talk to your spouse. Next time you feel sexually aroused, don't massage your friend. Wait until you're home with your spouse. If you have to go to the corporate retreat, don't go alone. Ask if you can bring your spouse. If you're surfing the Internet and your spouse comes home, don't stay online. Turn off your computer and connect with your spouse.

Your soul is indivisible. It can't be shared. You have to preserve it for one person. It's like a long-distance telephone provider. You have to pick one. You have to offer someone an exclusive.

Your primal yearning for connection originates partially from the unity you experienced with your mother. Your quest for love is your quest to replicate that experience. You had one mother. You can only have one soul mate.

The problem that most people have is not that they don't know how to connect; it's that they don't know how to limit their connection with others and preserve their soul for their spouse. Step four of the MarriageMax™ 4-Step Plan for building phenomenal love is to *save yourself* for your spouse.

Caution: Same-Sex Friends

It's obvious that you cannot connect with your spouse if either of you are having an affair. By now you're more aware

Save Yourself Marriage Assessment

Answer "yes" or "no" to the following questions and compare your score to the assessment scale below.

		Yes	No
1.	Do you have opposite sex close personal friendships?	☐	☐
2.	Do you have same-sex close personal friends with whom you regularly share your feelings or intimate details about your life?	☐	☐
3.	Do you keep in touch with ex-lovers?	☐	☐
4.	Do you share your personal life with colleagues or clients?	☐	☐
5.	Do you flirt?	☐	☐
6.	Do you fantasize about anyone other than your spouse?	☐	☐
7.	Have you ever been unfaithful?	☐	☐
8.	Do you have a hobby, interest, game, sport, or activity that interferes with your connection to your spouse?	☐	☐
9.	Is there anyone besides your spouse that you have physical contact with regularly?	☐	☐
10.	Do you have any family members with whom you regularly share your feelings or intimate details about your life?	☐	☐

	Yes	No
11. Is there anyone other than your spouse that you give to regularly?	☐	☐
12. Do you dress provocatively?	☐	☐
13. Do you have any addictions?	☐	☐
14. Do you ever share good news with someone before sharing it with your spouse?	☐	☐
15. If an attractive person flirted with you, would you engage them and enjoy it?	☐	☐

Total number of "yes" answers: ☐

0–3. MARRIAGE FITNESS CHAMPION. You are physically, emotionally, and spiritually faithful to your spouse. Congratulations. Still, ask yourself if you fall short in any area or if you have room to improve and continue to work on it.

4–8. AVERAGE. You could *save yourself* a lot more and intensify the connection with your spouse. You're probably not aware of how damaging the connections you are making outside your marriage are to the relationship with your spouse.

9–15. OUT OF SHAPE. Your focus is outside your marriage. You are borderline unfaithful to your spouse, either physically or emotionally, or both. You need to redirect your focus to what's most important. Quit all the extracurricular. It's draining your marriage.

of the problem with emotional infidelity too. And I think we all know at least one marriage that broke up because someone was obsessed with work, a hobby, drugs, alcohol, or food. In many cases, it's easy to see how a connection outside your marriage interferes with your love. But the potential problem with same-sex friendships warrants its own discussion.

Conventional wisdom says that same-sex friendships are harmless to your marriage. But if infidelity can be emotional or sexual, then you can be unfaithful with a man or a woman. If a deep connection to work, a hobby, drugs, alcohol, or food—inanimate things—can occupy a person's soul, then so can anyone, regardless of their gender.

I know two women who think they're friends, but they're really soul mates. They talk on the phone incessantly and share their most private thoughts about everything from sex and money to addictions and personal hygiene. They speak to each other immediately upon waking and before going to bed. They are completely tuned-in to every aspect of each other's lives.

Their friendship fulfills their strong desire for intimacy, but it ruins any chance of them connecting with their husbands. There's no room for their husbands in their souls. They're filled up with each other. They tell each other everything. They never want to tell the same story twice. Even when they tell their husband too, it's not the same as when they tell each other. The second person told is… second. They feel excited to tell each other. They feel obligated to tell their husbands. Where do you think they connect?

Friendship can offer intimacy but not ultimate fulfillment. Only love can complete you. And to create love, your soul has to be completely available.

There's nothing wrong with healthy friendships that include occasional personal discussions and thoughtful gestures, but you should not make a soul connection with anyone other than your spouse. If you think you have a friendship that interferes with your marriage, change it. Stop doing the things that connect you deeply. Don't stop being friends. Just stop being emotional lovers. Free your soul. Make yourself available for your spouse.

How to Love Your Parents *and* Your Spouse

Chapter 1 discussed the original connection you had with your mother, your gradual separation, and your subsequent yearning to connect with someone else of the opposite sex. The process of growing up includes separating from your parents because it is a prerequisite for finding true love as an adult. The problem that some people have connecting with their spouse is that they never sufficiently separate from their mother or father.

When you closed the big deal or got the big promotion, who did you call first to share the news? I know someone who called his mother instead of his wife. It wasn't a calculated decision. It was a reaction based on his connection to his mom. That phone call told much more than good news. It was telling about a problem in his marriage. He was not available to his wife because he was connected to his mother.

Some people speak to one of their parents a couple of times each day. There is nothing inherently problematic about speaking to a parent frequently, but sometimes people's connection to a parent interferes with their connection to their spouse. If someone had a similar connection with a friend of the opposite sex, I might advise that they stop speaking. Of course, I would never suggest not speaking to a parent, but an adjustment to a child-parent relationship is sometimes necessary for the benefit of one's marriage.

The Bible says, "A man should leave his father and mother, bond with his wife, and become one flesh." This refers not only to a physical departure but an emotional separation too. Why doesn't the Bible just recommend bonding with your spouse? Why does it recommend "leaving" your parents too? Because one is not possible without the other. To deeply connect with your spouse, you first have to "leave" your parents.

Of course, I am not suggesting that you shouldn't have a healthy relationship with your parents. The Bible also says that you should honor your mother and father (it's one of the Ten Commandments). But the question is—what is a "healthy" relationship with your parents? Since that's not the subject of this book, I'll answer the question by stating what a healthy relationship with your parents is *not*. It's not one that includes a deep soul connection. That's the goal of your relationship with your spouse, and your soul needs to be completely available to accomplish it.

What's the nature of your relationship with your mother and father? Do you think your relationship with either of them interferes with your connection to your spouse? If so, how can you modify your relationship so that it's healthy and respectful without it occupying your soul?

Hold Back (Exercise 4.1)

Physical fitness isn't just about adding elements that improve your health, like exercise and more fruits and vegetables. It's also about subtracting elements that are not compatible with your goal. Could you really call yourself "healthy" if you exercised faithfully but continued to smoke or eat at fast food restaurants? Marriage Fitness, like physical fitness, asks you to stop certain activities that are unhealthy for your marriage.

I want to warn you. You may find the five exercises below more difficult than the exercises in the rest of the MarriageMax™ 4-Step Plan. The other exercises in the MarriageMax 4-Step Plan ask you to *do* something. The five exercises below ask you to refrain from doing things. As difficult as it is to begin a new discipline, it's usually more difficult to break old habits. However, the more you succeed implementing the exercises already discussed, the easier it will be for you to implement the five exercises below.

As is the case with the entire MarriageMax™ 4-Step Plan, to succeed with *save yourself* requires a consistent consciousness. I suggest you review this chapter regularly, listen to audio productions on the topic, attend lectures and seminars, learn it with your spouse, meditate on the idea, and talk about it with your friends and family. I also recommend *Emotional Infidelity* by M. Gary Neuman. *Emotional Infidelity* is an excellent book that discusses comprehensively the topic of this chapter.

On the other hand, you cannot rely exclusively on the right attitude. Correct thinking is not enough to create love. You need a discipline to help you actualize your intentions. Here are five exercises for you to employ that will help you *save yourself*.

When I lived in New York City, I bought the newspaper from the same street vendor everyday. In the thirty seconds it took to complete the transaction, we chatted briefly about the weather or last Sunday's football game. We spoke to each other everyday, but we never developed a connection.

On the other hand, on our first date, my wife and I talked for hours about each other's family dynamics, career dreams, and personal problems. We made a connection in just one evening.

When you spend time with someone, there is the *possibility* for a connection, but it won't happen unless you share your inner lives. People connect when they share thoughts, feelings, fears, hopes, and dreams. No one ever fell in love talking about the stock market.

Life requires you to relate to many people: your boss, your barber, your manicurist, your housekeeper, your butcher, your accountant, your neighbors, your family, your friends, the librarian, your clients, and salespeople. You should strive to have productive and healthy relationships with everyone in your life. But be careful not to get too personal. Don't talk about your problems or ask for personal advice. If you need to have a personal discussion with someone, try to include your spouse. If that's not possible, limit the frequency of your discussions with this person. Save your inner life for your spouse. Be careful not to connect outside your marriage.

Some people go to the hair salon for a therapy session. They might argue that no one listens to them at home so why does it matter what they reveal during their appointment? But it does matter because in order to connect with your spouse you have to be available. If you're not available, then of course your spouse won't want to listen. In the depths of your spouse's desires is a need to connect. If your spouse senses that listening will connect you, they might listen. If not, they won't be interested.

Everyone needs an outlet for their personal problems and feelings. But it shouldn't be on the racquetball court with your friend. Your spouse should be your outlet. Where you reveal yourself is where you will connect yourself. *Save yourself* for your spouse.

The more you *hold back* with others, the more you will need your spouse. You won't talk to your spouse because you feel obligated; you'll talk because you need to talk. And you'll connect with your spouse because you *saved yourself* for them.

Of course, this works best when both spouses are tuned-in to the exercise. If one spouse is saving themselves, but the other is not physically or emotionally available, then *hold back* will be more challenging. In this case, I recommend holding back as much as possible anyway, keeping your soul available and encouraging your spouse to learn about *put love first,* step one of the MarriageMax™ 4-Step Plan. Then your spouse might step into the space you made available for them.

There will be plenty of times when you will feel that you need advice or input from other people who offer a unique perspective or particular expertise. I'm not suggesting that you should never consult with others. But consult with your spouse first. Think about whether or not you really need additional input. And when you do consult with others, be sensitive to whether or not you are approaching them for advice or to connect. It's very common for people to reach out to others under the guise of seeking counsel when, in fact, they are seeking to connect.

My wife and I look forward to our *talk charges, super talk charges, date nights, romantic retreats, business meetings,* and *what do you think* opportunities. We rarely reveal our inner lives to anyone except each other, so we need time to talk. Sometimes I can't wait to talk to my wife because I have a lot on my mind or I need advice. I need an outlet. I talk to her and it's with her that I connect.

Do you share your inner life with someone other than your spouse? Do you do it occasionally or does this person serve as a regular outlet for you? Is there a compelling reason why you need to share your problems or feelings with anyone other than your spouse or could you *hold back?* If there is someone other than your spouse with whom you think you have a connection, talk with this person about your desire to connect with your spouse and explain why you need to *hold back.* Now turn to your spouse.

Please Do Not Touch (Exercise 4.2)

There's an insightful scene in the movie *Doctor Zhivago.* Lara boards an electric trolley, walks toward the rear of the car, and brushes shoulders with Doctor Zhivago. Their heads turn and their eyes meet. They feel something special. The camera cuts to the sparking wires above the trolley.

This scene is effective because the writer and the director know that everyone can relate to Lara and Doctor Zhivago's encounter. A simple touch can be electrifying.

One day I saw an old friend in a restaurant. He shared with me that he was engaged to be married. I congratulated him and asked him how he met his fiancé. He said that she came into his office and made an appointment with him for a massage. I asked him when they were getting married, and that's when the story got more complicated.

They didn't have a wedding date because she was still married to another man. I cautiously asked him if he was sure he wanted to marry a woman whom he met while she was in the throes of a divorce. He corrected me and explained that when they met, she was content with her marriage. She was not in the throes of a divorce. But after a few sessions with him, they could not deny the electrifying energy between them. From the moment he laid his hands on her, something magical happened. A passionate love affair evolved. Finally, she decided to divorce her husband and marry my friend.

As discussed in Chapter 4, touch is more energizing to a relationship than most people realize. Affairs do not begin with two people lying naked in bed. They begin with a gentle rub, a harmless kiss, or a warm hug. You don't have to massage someone's entire body to make a connection with them. Just as a *touch charge* with your spouse sends power to your core, touching someone else sends it away.

Touch is like glue—it bonds. If it were a product, it would need a warning on its package. "Use with caution, bonds instantly. Has no regard for circumstances or appropriateness." In the song *He Touched Me,* Barbra Streisand sings "Suddenly, nothing is the same." She understands the power of touch.

Making physical contact with a person is like making a deposit into a bank account. Something builds up between you. And the more you touch that person, the more invested you are in them. Furthermore, like a deposit, you can only make it into one bank. If you invest your touch with someone else, your marriage gets shortchanged.

Your soul is like one side of a zipper; there's only one counterpart. Touch is one way to zip up with your counterpart. The more you touch someone else, the more you zip up with them. The less physical contact you have outside your marriage, the more you will be available to your spouse.

This may seem like a strange idea to you at first. It certainly conflicts with social norms which allow casual touching, hugging, and kissing. In many environments, it's even acceptable to be overtly sexual. But in most environments, it's also normal to get divorced.

If you're skeptical, test it for yourself. Monitor your feelings when you touch or are touched. Take an honest sur-

vey of some friends. Do you really feel nothing when someone puts their arm around you? When you get your hair
washed at the salon, is it the same experience regardless of
who washes it? Or do you feel something different if it's an
attractive person of the opposite sex? Did you ever get a professional massage? Do you have a preference for a man or a
woman? Why?

It's normal to have desire for physical contact with the
opposite sex. It's also normal for some of that desire to be
satisfied by what most people would consider socially
acceptable touching, hugging, and kissing. But if you *save
yourself* for your spouse, and release all that sexual energy
with them—wow!

I try not to have physical contact with any woman
except my wife. I get my hair cut by a man and when I greet
women, I don't hug or kiss them. My wife doesn't ever wonder about any social contact I have with other women or
where it might lead. She also doesn't worry that I won't
desire her. I'm human and she's my only outlet. Of course,
I'm attracted to her anyway—that's one reason I proposed.
But this ensures that my physical desires, which could be partially met by other woman through socially acceptable contact, are channeled one hundred percent toward my wife.

This practice occasionally interferes slightly with relationships I have with other women, but I believe that having
socially acceptable physical contact with other women
would interfere with my marriage. In other words, I have a
choice—compromise my marriage with my wife or the relationships I have with other women. For me, it's an easy
choice. And in the long run, my relationships with other
women are better too. In almost all cases, the women I know
understand and respect the sanctity I extend to my wife and
our marriage. In fact, I believe they want their husbands to
extend the same exclusivity to them.

Limiting physical contact to your spouse probably
seems like a strange idea. But that's only because you don't
do it. Here's my suggestion—try it. Limit your physical

contact to your spouse for one week. For one week, don't touch, rub, hug, or kiss anyone of the opposite sex (except your children and your parents). If you need to explain yourself to anyone, either tell them about your experiment or say that you have a cold. Then, unleash all your stored-up energy with your spouse.

This One's For You (Exercise 4.3)

As discussed in Chapter 5, giving creates a connection to the person to whom you give. Therefore, it's important to guard the frequency with which you give to anyone other than your spouse.

I know a man and a woman who regularly forward to each other one-liners or jokes that are emailed to them. They share the same sense of humor, and these email exchanges are the basis for their constant contact. Every once in a while, they send it to their spouses too, but it's an afterthought and their spouses know it. These gestures appear harmless, but they are cultivating a connection that crowds out their spouses.

Instead of sharing these one-liners and jokes with each other, they should share them with their spouses. Their spouses may not appreciate the jokes as much, but they will appreciate the connection much more.

Are you giving presents or your presence to anyone regularly other than your spouse? Are you forwarding emails or mailing articles to someone else? Do you buy flowers or thoughtful gifts for someone else? Do you feel a connection with anyone you give to regularly? If so, redirect those *gives* to your spouse.

TV Fast (Exercise 4.4)

"Honey, can I talk to you?" she said.

"Wait until a commercial," he mumbles.

"What's wrong?" she inquires.

"Nothing," he says. "I'm just trying to watch a program."

"It's after 10 p.m. I haven't seen or spoken to you all day, and the kids are finally asleep," she responds. "Can you talk to me for a minute?"

"What do you want to talk about?" he says without taking his eyes off the TV.

"Could you turn the TV off?" she asks in desperation.

"Fine," he says as he reluctantly turns it off. "What do you want?"

Whether this resembles an occasional evening dialogue in your house or not, the TV is probably interfering to some extent with your marriage and the intimacy you might otherwise have with your spouse. Let's face it—if you're facing the TV, you're turned away from each other.

Do you or your spouse collapse in front of the TV at the end of the day? Do you fight about which program to watch? Do you battle over control for the clicker? Are you sure the TV is bringing you pleasure? Or is it causing you pain?

Even though the TV is in front of you, more often than not, in the case of marriages, it comes between you. People get very into their TV programs and sporting events. Talk about connecting—sometimes people are so connected to what they're watching that they don't even hear their spouse speaking to them.

Talk with your spouse about experimenting with a *TV fast*—one week with no TV. Use the time to turn toward each other.

My wife and I tried this and decided to get rid of the TV's in our home. I would have to write a separate book to describe the magnitude of the positive impact that I believe that decision has had on our marriage, our children, and our entire family life. Before you jump to do the same, try a week-long *TV fast*. At the end of the week, review with your spouse how you felt about not watching any TV. How was your life different? What was the effect on your marriage? Discuss what actions you might want to take based on your conclusions.

Dress for Success (Exercise 4.5)

There's an expression, "It's business, not personal." And the two *are* different.

A business woman probably has two types of clothes in her wardrobe. She has conservative clothes for work and a strapless dress for certain personal occasions.

Why wouldn't a woman wear a strapless dress to a business meeting? Because it's not good to mix business and pleasure. A strapless dress is too personal for business. Wearing it would facilitate an emotional connection with her colleagues instead of a professional one. A conservative outfit, on the other hand, promotes a more detached business-like relationship.

Do you see how the mood of a relationship is established before anyone says a word? Two people connect or keep their emotional distance depending on how they dress. The more provocative your attire, the more you connect with people of the opposite sex. But connecting with others interferes with your connection to your spouse. As soon as someone looks at you with desire, you begin to connect with them. And usually both people feel it—the one who looked, and the one who was gazed upon.

You don't have to talk or touch to begin a core connection. The eyes are the window to the soul.

Dress for success means not to dress provocatively (except when you're in private with your spouse) in order to avoid extramarital connections. I'm not saying you shouldn't look good, dress fine, and be well-groomed. The issue is whether or not your attire is provoking an emotional connection or the appropriate distance from the opposite sex. Less provocative dress maintains the appropriate distance and safeguards your soul.

How do you know if your attire is provocative? There are a couple of clues. If your intent when you get dressed is to display your body or attract attention to yourself, then you're probably on the wrong track. If your outfit reveals parts of your body that people usually only see in advertisements for intimate apparel, you've crossed the line. If you have to lie on your bed in order to button your pants, then you might want to consider buying the next size. You should strive to dress well—refined and attractive—but not provocatively.

My wife, for example, dresses very stylishly and always looks great. She just doesn't wear mini-skirts, halter tops, deep v-necks, or tight pants. I'm sure men think she's "put-together," well-groomed, and beautiful, but her dress, like the wedding ring on her finger, sends a clear message about her availability. And that is her intent.

The same principle applies to men's clothing. I encourage physical fitness as well as Marriage Fitness, but men should not wear clothes that show off their muscles or otherwise might provoke women to connect with them.

Think of your appearance as a sort of "red light-green light" message to the opposite sex. What message are you sending? Is your appearance causing you to connect with people other than your spouse? How are your fashion choices affecting your marriage?

Most people's wardrobe choices are motivated by fashion trends and peer pressure. But think about it. What mood is your clothing setting for your relationships? Are you trying to solicit an emotional reaction with your fashion choices? Are you trying to attract others or are you *saving yourself* for your spouse?

Do you get a thrill being noticed by people? Is it exciting to have someone look at your body? Do you thrive on attention? You can still have your thrill, but get it from your spouse. Let your spouse satisfy your need. You only need to turn one head. Tell your spouse—"This is for your eyes only." And put on something no one else gets to see you wear.

Some men unbutton their shirt and loosen their tie after work before they go home. What does that say about whom they are trying to impress? If you're a man, what about doing the reverse? Before you come home, button your top button, knot your tie, and brush your hair. The woman you want to look best for is home, not at the office.

You can look good without being provocative. There's no reason to hide your attractiveness. But there's every reason to cover your body and safeguard your soul. *Dress for success*—don't dress provocatively. *Save yourself* for your spouse.

Summary

True love is a combination of initiating certain actions and ceasing from other actions. Step four of the MarriageMax™ 4-Step Plan is to *save yourself*—to cease from certain behaviors that interfere with you connecting to your spouse.

You can't share your soul with someone else and still have true love with your spouse. Here are five exercises to help ensure that your soul is available to your spouse.

1. *Hold back.* Don't share your inner life with anyone except your spouse.

2. *Please do not touch.* Touch creates a bond between people. For at least one week, don't touch anyone of the opposite sex other than your spouse, your parents, and your children.

3. *This one's for you.* Don't give your presence to anyone other than your spouse.

4. *TV fast.* Don't watch TV for one week. Then discuss with your spouse a new TV frequency policy for your home.

5. *Dress for success.* Don't dress provocatively.

Conclusion

Y   ou now have a four step Marriage Fitness program
    that includes twenty exercises. Like any fitness pro-
    gram, the key to success is consistency. Going on a
diet for a few weeks accomplishes nothing, but changing
your eating habits can transform your health. The same
principle applies in Marriage Fitness. To succeed, you have
to be consistent. The four steps and the twenty exercises
have to become part of your lifestyle.

Below is a fourteen week implementation schedule
designed to make Marriage Fitness part of your lifestyle. The
four steps and the twenty exercises discussed in this book are
too much for anyone to implement into their marriage
immediately. It has to be done gradually. Like all great feats,
it's accomplished one small step at a time. The schedule
below will help you take those steps and lead you to full
implementation.

Successful Implementation

There are four keys to successfully incorporating Marriage
Fitness into your lifestyle:

1.   Begin now

2.   Go slow

3.   Own it

4.   Keep implementing

The first key is to begin. Take action now. Reading,

thinking, contemplating, discussing—it's all good, but if you want to make a difference in your marriage, you must *do*.

If for some reason, you're not thrilled with the schedule suggested below, make your own. But whatever you do, begin now. Take the first step. Begin at least one exercise today!

The second key is to go slow. The quickest way to fail with the entire plan is to fail with the first part of the plan. Start small so you can succeed and feel good about your efforts.

A friend of mine is inspired periodically to begin exercising. He means well and intends to change his lifestyle, but in his excitement he lifts more weights in his first work out than he should lift in an entire month. He's so sore afterwards he can't return to the gym for the rest of the week. His inspiration turns to discouragement and he quits.

Treat yourself to positive reinforcement. Start small and succeed with whatever you do.

The third key is to "own it" before you progress. It's not enough to succeed with an exercise for a day or two. You have to make sure you "own it" before you add more steps or exercises to your Marriage Fitness program. Every exercise and step has to become part of your lifestyle so that your success won't be jeopardized when you increase your program. The below schedule is a guide. If you don't feel ready to move on when the schedule suggests, then don't. Add to your program only after you "own" everything you've started.

The fourth key is to keep implementing more exercises and steps until the entire MarriageMax™ 4-Step Plan is part of your lifestyle. In other words, keep moving. Don't let your Marriage Fitness program get stale. Don't stall before full implementation. As soon as you "own" what you're doing, do more.

A Fourteen Week Implementation Schedule

Week	Step	Exercise	Page
1	Put Love First	1.1 Talk Charges 1.5 Schedule Romantic Retreat 1.7 Photo Opp.	82 88 93
2	Put Love First	1.3 Touch Charges	85
3	Put Love First	1.4 Date Night	86
4	Put Love First	1.2 Super Talk Charges	84
5	Put Love First	1.6 Business Meeting	91
6	Give Presence	2.1 Intimacy Interviews	112
7	Give Presence	2.2 Gives	116
8	Move from Me to We	3.1 Move Your Circle of Life	133
9	Move from Me to We	3.2 Pick a Hobby—any Hobby 3.3 Make Room for Love	136 137
10	Move from Me to We	3.4 Be a Team 3.5 What Do You Think?	143 149
11	Save Yourself	4.1 Hold Back	162
12	Save Yourself	4.2 Please Do Not Touch	165
13	Save Yourself	4.3 This One's for You 4.4 TV Fast	168 168
14	Save Yourself	4.5 Dress for Success	170

To be scheduled: Don't forget the *Birthday Party*. (Page 93)

The Love Contract

My wife and I once got a call from a real estate broker who had a prospective buyer for our house. In the ensuing months, this couple visited the house three times (once with their parents), hired an appraiser and an attorney, met with me personally to discuss some issues, spoke with the broker no less than ten times, and made a verbal offer which we accepted. The due diligence process with this prospective buyer was as extensive as it gets in residential real estate. However, they didn't sign the contract. They wanted the house. They probably already discussed where they would put their furniture. But without a signed contract, the deed still said "Fertel" and they still lived in a rental.

Your signature changes everything.

Below is a *Love Contract* for your consideration. I encourage you to sign it. Your signature can reflect your commitment, or you can invite your spouse to sign as well and make it a contract between the two of you.

If you really want to transform your marriage, it's not enough to know more about love—you have to *do* more about love. Commit to do. Sign below.

You may not want to sign the contract as is. Feel free to edit it for any reason to fit your needs.

I, the undersigned, hereby agree to *put love first*—to make my spouse and my marriage the absolute highest priority in my life bar none. I also agree to *give presence* and *move from me to we*. I understand that step four *(save yourself)* is necessary to achieve the yin-yang balance of love and I commit to implementing this step too.

Specifically, I commit to the following exercises (check your choices below) based on the schedule recommended above or an amended schedule of my choice.

Step 1: Put Love First

___ Talk Charge: five per day

___ Super Talk Charge: 25 minutes once per week

___ Touch Charge: three per day

___ Date Night: once per week

___ Romantic Retreat: three per year

___ Business Meeting: once per week

___ Photo Opp.

___ Birthday Party

Step 2: Give Presence

___ Intimacy Interview

___ Give: three per day

Step 3: Move from Me to We

___ Move Your Circle of Life

___ Pick a Hobby—any Hobby

___ Make Room for Love

___ Be a Team

___ What Do You Think?

Step 4: Save Yourself

___ Hold Back

___ Please Do Not Touch

___ This One's for You

___ TV Fast

___ Dress for Success

_____   _____
Spouse 1(print name)   Spouse 1 (signature)

Date_____

_____   _____
Spouse 2 (print name)   Spouse 2 (signature)

Date_____

Full summary

Marriage Fitness is like physical fitness. It gets your marriage in shape. Marriage Fitness solves existing problems, prevents future problems, and unleashes a powerful energy in your life.

Love is the most awesome experience in life because it fulfills our most basic need—the need to connect with another person. But falling in love is a gift from Mother Nature which doesn't last forever. When love fades from your relationship, so does the ecstasy from your life. You also experience flaws in your spouse and incompatibilities in your relationship. But neither your spouse nor your compatibility changed. Your love changed, and that changed your experience of everything.

Make the choice to connect again with your spouse. You connected deeply when you fell in love. You can do it again. This time it won't be a gift. You'll have to make it happen. But when you do—when you reconnect—everything will change "from frog to prince."

Love is a golden lens through which life looks wonderful. Love quenches your deepest desire and it is there that you find ultimate fulfillment in marriage and in life.

There are two parts to your existence.

1. Your character, which is the role you play in life. Your character is everything you know about yourself including your character traits, personality, appearance, health, career, physique, social life, family life, finances, abilities, disposition, and your outlook on life.

2. Your soul. This is your essential self—the core of your existence.

Your character changes over time like compact discs in a player. However, your soul never changes. It experiences the changes of your character but remains constant. It's fixed while your character is in flux. It's like the compact disc player.

This distinction is crucial because in order to make the

connection with your spouse that transforms your marriage and your life, you have to know what to connect. Character compatibility is nice, but it has very little to do with true love. On the other hand, when you and your spouse become soul mates—when you connect at the core of your existence—the golden lens appears and your marriage and your life are transformed forever. True love is about becoming soul mates—not role mates.

Becoming soul mates requires effort. It takes time and energy. True love is a verb, not a feeling. There are four steps to building and maintaining love in your marriage.

Step one of the MarriageMax™ 4-Step Plan is to make your spouse and your marriage the absolute highest priority in your life bar none. In other words, step one is to *put love first*. *Put love first* is a prerequisite for all the other steps. Your marriage has to be the highest priority in your life in order for you to have the time and energy for steps two, three, and four.

There are eight exercises to help you *put love first*.

Exercise 1.1: *Talk charge.* Have loving personal talks with your spouse five times each day for a minimum of one minute.

Exercise 1.2: *Super talk charge.* Have a loving personal talk with your spouse once each week for a minimum of twenty-five minutes.

Exercise 1.3: *Touch charge.* Make loving physical contact with your spouse a minimum of three times each day.

Exercise 1.4: *Date night.* Go out alone on a date with your spouse at least once each week.

Exercise 1.5: *Romantic retreat.* Go on vacation at least three times per year alone with your spouse for at least three days and two nights.

Exercise 1.6: *Business meeting.* Avoid as many logistical and business discussions throughout the week as possible and discuss all of them during a weekly *business meeting*.

Exercise 1.7: *Photo opp.* Put photos of your spouse in your wallet, your office, and your gym locker.

Exercise 1.8: *Birthday party*. Plan an extravagant birthday party for your spouse. Invite only your spouse.

The second step in the MarriageMax™ 4-Step Plan is to *give presence*. You're probably accustomed to the feeling of love inspiring you to give to your spouse. But the correlation between love and giving works the other way too. In other words, giving builds a connection between you and your spouse and creates the experience of love. And ironically, when you give, you get everything you need.

There are two exercises to help you *give presence*.

Exercise 2.1: *Intimacy interview*. Extensively interview your spouse in order to create an inventory of giving opportunities.

Exercise 2.2: *Give*. *Give* from your inventory at least three times per day.

Step three of the MarriageMax™ 4-Step Plan for connecting your cores is to embrace your spouse's shortcomings, uniqueness, and challenges. Step three is to *move from me to we*—to get involved in each other's lives.

When you marry, you choose your spouse, but that choice includes the future of your spouse who you don't yet know—your fate. And to succeed in love, you have to commit to both—Rachel *and* Leah, your choice *and* your fate, the revealed *and* the unrevealed.

Here are five exercises to help you *move from me to we*.

Exercise 3.1: *Move your circle of life*. Get more involved in one of your spouse's hobbies or interests.

Exercise 3.2: *Pick a hobby—any hobby*. You and your spouse select a hobby to do together.

Exercise 3.3: *Make room for love*. Select one of your hobbies or interests that your spouse is not involved with and eliminate it from your life.

Exercise 3.4: *Be a team*. Invite your spouse to help you fix one of your problems or flaws.

Exercise 3.5: *What do you think?* Ask your spouse their opinion before making decisions.

True love is a combination of initiating certain actions and ceasing from other actions. Step four of the Marriage Max™ 4-Step Plan is to *save yourself*—to cease from certain behaviors that interfere with connecting to your spouse.

You can't share your soul with someone else and still have true love with your spouse. Here are five exercises to help ensure that your soul is available to your spouse.

Exercise 4.1: *Hold back.* Refrain from sharing your inner life with anyone other than your spouse.

Exercise 4.2: *Please do not touch.* Refrain from physical contact with anyone of the opposite sex other than your spouse, your parents, and your children.

Exercise 4.3: *This one's for you.* Refrain from regularly giving gifts to or having thoughtful correspondence with anyone other than your spouse.

Exercise 4.4: *TV fast.* A minimum of once a year, turn off the television for an entire week.

Exercise 4.5: *Dress for success.* Refrain from dressing in a way that will provoke an emotional connection from the opposite sex (except in private with your spouse).

The End and the Beginning

Creating love in your marriage is the most important accomplishment you can achieve in your life. A strong marriage enhances every other area of your life and is the only achievement that can offer you ultimate fulfillment. *If you and your spouse become soul mates, you will have everything. If you do not, nothing else will be enough.* You could have money, cars, clothes, jewelry, friends, power, fame, intelligence, wit, family, strength, and beauty—but if you do not deeply connect with your spouse, you will squander the potential of your marriage and your life.

Like your physical fitness, the health of your marriage deserves serious attention. The MarriageMax™ 4-Step Plan can help you get into shape and realize the potential of your marriage and your life.

You're at the end of this book, but the beginning of Marriage Fitness for you. Just as with physical fitness, reading a book about Marriage Fitness only works if you translate what you read into your life. Inspiration is a lot more common than discipline. Implement what you learned now! And for more inspiration as well as opportunities for other Marriage Fitness programs including audio CD's, a free newsletter, free lectures, marriage coaching, and live seminars, visit www.marriagemax.com.

Love is *not* a mystery. Like your physical fitness, the success of your marriage is governed by universal laws. MARRIAGE FITNESS translates these laws into four simple steps:

The MarriageMax™ 4-Step Plan

1. Put Love First
2. Give Presence
3. Move from Me to We
4. Save Yourself

I did not invent the universal laws of love, but MARRIAGE FITNESS organizes them so you can harness their power in your marriage. The laws of love are like the laws of gravity. They hold you back until you understand them. Then you can go to the moon. The MarriageMax™ 4-Step Plan is like rocket boosters. Now you can go to phenomenal love. Enjoy the journey.

Mort Fertel
mortfertel@marriagemax.com
www.marriagemax.com

WHAT'S NEXT?

**Get the FREE Breakthrough Report
"7 Secrets for Staying on Track"**

Exclusively for readers of
MARRIAGE FITNESS

This free report is packed with NEW insights,
stories, and tips guaranteed to keep you inspired
and headed in the right direction. "7 Secrets for
Staying on Track" fills in the gaps and gives you a
surprisingly simple step-by-step follow-up guide.

Don't delay. Sign up now at
www.YourMarriageFitness.com/StayOnTrack
(It's absolutely FREE.)

Private 1-On-1 Sessions
with Mort Fertel

Phone sessions, office visits,
or full day intensive "house calls."

For more information and a fee schedule, please visit
www.MortFertel.com/Marriage-Coaching.asp

To make an appointment, please call 410.764.1552.

Need a speaker for an upcoming event?
Want to bring the message of Marriage Fitness
to your community LIVE?

Speaking Services by Mort Fertel

When you hire Mort Fertel, you get it all—
an electrifying presentation and groundbreaking
content. His seminars are an incredible blend of
meaning and magic. Everyone will be entertained,
inspired, and walk away with an indelible message
that will improve their marriage forever.

Mort Fertel is an ideal speaker for:
- Special Events
- Executive Education
- Keynote Speeches
- Conferences
- Retreats
- Non-profit Programs
- Professional Meetings

Various formats available including:
- 15 minute power talk
- 30 minute keynote
- 50 minute program
- 3 hour seminar experience
- Full day workshop
- Multi-day retreats

For more information, visit www.MarriageMax.com